OXF(
INDI
INTRODUCTIONS

SURROGACY

The Oxford India Short
Introductions are concise,
stimulating, and accessible guides
to different aspects of India.
Combining authoritative analysis,
new ideas, and diverse perspectives,
they discuss subjects which are
topical yet enduring, as also
emerging areas of study and debate.

OTHER TITLES IN THE SERIES

Jawaharlal Nehru
Rudrangshu Mukherjee

The Partition of India
Haimanti Roy

Indian Nuclear Policy
Harsh V. Pant and Yogesh Joshi

Indian Democracy
Suhas Palshikar

Indian National Security
Chris Ogden

Business, Institutions, Environment
Runa Sarkar

Public Policy in India
Rajesh Chakrabarti and Kaushiki Sanyal

Bollywood
M.K. Raghavendra

The Indian Middle Class
Surinder S. Jodhka and Aseem Prakash

Indian Foreign Policy
Sumit Ganguly

Dalit Assertion
Sudha Pai

For more information, visit our website:
https://india.oup.com/content/series/o/
oxford-india-short-introductions/

OXFORD
INDIA SHORT
INTRODUCTIONS

SURROGACY

ANINDITA MAJUMDAR

OXFORD
UNIVERSITY PRESS

OXFORD
UNIVERSITY PRESS

Oxford University Press is a department of the University of Oxford.
It furthers the University's objective of excellence in research, scholarship,
and education by publishing worldwide. Oxford is a registered trademark of
Oxford University Press in the UK and in certain other countries.

Published in India by
Oxford University Press
2/11 Ground Floor, Ansari Road, Daryaganj, New Delhi 110 002, India

ISBN-13 (print edition): 978-0-19-949279-4
ISBN-10 (print edition): 0-19-949279-4

ISBN-13 (eBook): 978-0-19-909654-1
ISBN-10 (eBook): 0-19-909654-6

Typeset in 11/14.3 Bembo Std
by The Graphics Solution, New Delhi 110 092
Printed in India by Replika Press Pvt. Ltd

Contents

1

Introduction

In December 2011, Bollywood superstar Aamir Khan announced, in a carefully worded letter to the press and public, that he and his wife had had a son through a surrogate. The letter was a thank-you note to the general public and to their doctor for crucial support. Strangely though, the letter did not mention the surrogate who carried the baby for them. Her anonymity as the gestational surrogate seemed to be overwhelmingly present in her absence.

The conditions under which commercial surrogacy has come to exist in India is based on these key factors of anonymity and stigma. The woman who agrees to carry a couple's child for nine months is dependent upon anonymity to protect the couple's identity and hers. This anonymity is an important paradox of commercial surrogacy, which lies in the complicated terrain of infertility, technology, and intimate relationships. Since the advent of in vitro fertilization (IVF), surrogacy has changed its contours. The advent of assisted reproductive technologies, also known as ARTs, means that surrogacy can now be entered into without any form of sexual relationship. IVF, or the process of artificially fertilizing extracted eggs and sperm, has made it possible for the surrogate to carry the child through artificial insemination. This also means that surrogacy now involves more persons than just the couple and the surrogate. Now, clinicians, surrogates, and couples all form an important part of the process of giving birth to the child through assisted reproduction. Also involved are the sperm and egg donors whose services may be hired in case the couple is unable to donate their own gametes to the surrogacy arrangement. Thus, in displacing sexual relationships in the surrogacy arrangement, ART creates two forms of surrogacy.

The first, known as genetic surrogacy, involves the artificial insemination of the sperm of the father-to-be (or sperm donor) into the uterus of the surrogate through the process of intrauterine insemination (IUI). The IUI is a simpler form of ART involving the manual insertion of the extracted sperm via a catheter directly into the vagina of the woman seeking a pregnancy. In that sense it is closest to the natural procreative process. In genetic surrogacy, the surrogate

2

contributes her egg and carries the baby for the full term. One of the most famous cases of surrogacy—the Baby M case—involved a genetic surrogate, Mary Beth Whitehead. In the 1980s, Edward Stern and his wife entered a surrogacy contract with Mary Beth, where she was to undergo an IUI to carry the baby for the Sterns. However, as soon as the baby was born, Mary Beth disappeared with the child, thereby reneging on the contract. The Sterns went to court and the case travelled through various federal courts in the United States of America (USA) before visitation rights were granted to Mary Beth; the judgment thereby upheld elements of the contract and gave parental rights to the Sterns.

The Baby M case became an important case study for feminists, child rights activists, and legal scholars. The most important argument in favour of Mary Beth Whitehead was that she was the mother of the child, even though contractually she had relinquished parental rights. But the question that many asked was whether motherhood could be compromised through a contract?

In case of gestational surrogacy, the right to motherhood becomes contested. Here, the surrogate is not the only possible mother. Thanks to IVF, the egg of the adoptive mother, or an egg donor is fertilized with the sperm of the father-to-be or an anonymous sperm donor in a laboratory to produce an embryo.

This embryo is then transferred into the uterus of the surrogate. Thus, in popular imagery, the surrogate fulfils the role of the incubate or gestate; thus, the emergence of the contemporary: 'Wombs on rent'. Though derogatory, the contemporary moniker refers to the kind of conceptualization that the surrogate is subject to in the gestational surrogacy arrangement. Under these circumstances, designating the surrogate as 'mother' is controversial—considering the number of women involved in the role of the 'mother'. The anonymous egg donor is equally eligible to be a mother. However, while the status of the father may be disputed as well—if there is a sperm donor involved—more often than not, it is the mother's role that is under scrutiny. Gestational surrogacy has become the accepted form of surrogacy in many parts of the world—and in countries such as India, it is compulsorily endorsed by medical associations and clinics as per the mandatory requirements in the draft bill of the Indian Council of Medical Research (ICMR).

Since 2008, the ICMR has been at the helm of developing laws regarding the use of ARTs in India, including formulating regulatory mechanisms governing biomedical research. In 2010, the (Draft) Regulation of Assisted Reproductive Technologies Bill was circulated for public conversations and suggestions. The bill mentioned surrogacy and suggested important measures governing its arrangement in India. It effectively prohibits genetic surrogacy in favour of gestational surrogacy.

Along with the advent and enforced popularity of the gestational surrogacy arrangement has emerged the parallel practice of transnational surrogacy. It is important to note that transnational surrogacy has its own form and structure, which have emerged from the concurrent co-mingling of certain structural conditions. As a transnational commercial enterprise, commercial surrogacy in India has projected particular ideas, identities, and practices. Some of these elements are discussed in this introductory chapter to lay down the arguments for the book.

Local–Global Nature of Transnational Surrogacy

Surrogacy in India has rapidly become part of the landscape of international reproductive tourism. Reproductive or procreative tourism is part of the growing travel circuits of infertile couples—from the developed and developing world to economies with affordable infertility care such as India, Thailand, Mexico, and Brazil. Reproductive tourism also includes circuits of egg donors travelling across the world to donate their biogenetic matter for fertility procedures.

The demand for Caucasian eggs from Caucasian women is part of a parallel 'industry' that facilitates cryopreserved eggs/ovum to be transported across continents, as well as promotes reproductive tourism for egg donors on paid holidays to donate their bio matter.

The commercial gestational surrogacy arrangement, since 2013, has suffered from lower 'footfalls' of foreign couples due to a directive from the Ministry of Home Affairs, Government of India, which restricts access to everyone but foreign heterosexual couples, married for two years and unable to conceive. This meant that foreign gay couples cannot contract a surrogacy arrangement in India, leading to reduced transnational traffic. But ways of circumventing such a directive also emerged when news reports suggested that after the devastating Nepal earthquake in 2014, the Israeli government airlifted Israeli gay couples stranded with their newborns—born from Indian surrogates—but ignored the surrogates. The Nepalese government's ambiguous stand banned domestic surrogacy arrangements, but allowed 'externally' contracted arrangements to be fulfilled on its soil. This effectively helped Indian IVF clinics to facilitate surrogacy arrangements between Indian surrogates and foreign gay couples in Nepal, while meeting the demands of the Indian directive.

In India, commercial surrogacy, too, occupies this complicated terrain of reproductive tourism.

The transnational character of the arrangement is because infertile couples and individuals—gay and heterosexual—from across the world are attracted to come to India, largely due to cheap treatment options and the availability of even cheaper surrogacy services from Indian gestates. The surrogacy industry has also benefitted from the way the arrangement has been marketed across the world—through IVF agents and doctors. In the documentary *Made in India* (2010) by Vaishali Sinha and Rebecca Haimowitz, a transnational agency run by an Indian and based in the USA liaisons with clinics and couples to contract a surrogacy arrangement in India.

Commercial surrogacy in India operates through spaces of transnational ties that include local networks of IVF clinics, surrogacy agents, and surrogates. When trying to understand the transnational political economy of surrogacy in India, we notice an important focus on what Bharadwaj and Glasner (2009) call 'liminal third spaces' in their book on stem cell research in India. These 'liminal third spaces' emerge in the conflicted and multiple engagements that the local governments, cultures, practices, and people undertake in relation to the global and the transnational. In the exchange of bodies and genetic material across borders and boundaries, liminal third spaces become important sites of conflict and critique to existing norms and rules. IVF clinics, intended parents, and commercial surrogates operate in these liminal third spaces that form important networks to facilitate a commercial surrogacy arrangement. IVF and ARTs are both universal and localized. Unable to sustain universalized Western notions and engagements with IVF in ethnographic encounters in other parts of the globe, ARTs become subject to localized manifestations. Hence, ARTs take on 'mutating' characteristics, as Inhorn and Birenbaum–Carmeli (2008) mention, which differentiate between cultural experiences of IVF/ARTs.

A culture thus emerges around IVF and its use, thriving on aggressive marketing and advertising, which positions this technology as the only solution to replicate and recreate when faced with the failures of biology, manifest in the form of infertility. Infertility has been popularly represented as a 'lifestyle disease', impacting only a few who belong to the middle and upper-middle classes. Lifestyle choices such as late marriage, stress, and an inhospitable urban environment impact fertility. Stories of an infertility 'epidemic' amongst the educated urban middle class made it a disease that had to be countered fast.

Thus, infertility and its treatment are constructed and marketed to a largely urban clientele, disregarding patients and requirements in the semi-urban and rural sectors. As per a 2010 newspaper report by Durgesh

Nandan Jha, the IVF wing of a government hospital in Delhi was 'ailing' due to very few embryologists and even lesser equipment. This 'apathy' on the part of the state emerges from its health policy which places the responsibility of a burgeoning population on the shoulders of its poor and economically weak masses.

According to Sunita Reddy and Imrana Qadeer (2010), IVF and transnational commercial surrogacy are essential parts of the burgeoning new medical tourism industry in India. This industry caters to most major health services, including organ transplantation, intensive surgeries, and intensive care. Within this industry, the IVF culture occupies an important place in the procreative/reproductive tourism industry, which is now being spearheaded by the 'surrogacy industry'. The moniker 'industry' was first mentioned in a document by the Law Commission of India (2009) on regulating commercial surrogacy.

Within the notion of an 'industry' is the overwhelming fear of exploitation that dogs research on commercial surrogacy. For scholars such as Rayna Rapp (2011) and Arlie Hochschild (2011), commercial surrogacy is exploitative, and yet, it occupies the conflicted terrain of reproductive choice and agency. Anthropological work emerging from India provides a more nuanced reading of commercial surrogacy and surrogates. For instance, Vora (2013) speaks of the kind of marketability that the IVF clinics depend upon to attract foreign clientele, necessarily involved in extracting the maximum amount of 'labour' from Indian surrogates, even as they are positioned as needy and, therefore, requiring intervention through involvement in commercial surrogacy. Pande (2011) calls this 'a gift for global sisters', wherein foreigners are told they are doing a philanthropic good deed by supporting Indian surrogates.

In 2015, a controversial advertisement by the Japanese advertising and marketing agency Dentsu—on surrogacy in India—showcased the Indian surrogate in an exoticized rural setting, seeking to escape impoverishment by participating in a gestational surrogacy arrangement for a Japanese couple. The advertisement ends with the surrogate looking at an image of the baby on the couple's phone, as she never gets to see it post delivery. In a commentary on the advertisement, Sarojini et al. (2015) speak of how motherhood is projected through a transnational marketing of supply and demand for children.

In the ethnographic research conducted by Deepa V. et al. (2013), five 'sites' were studied to look at the particularities of commercial surrogacy in India. Besides Amritsar, Mumbai, Delhi, and Hyderabad, the world wide web forms the fifth site of surrogacy networks.

Each of the sites discussed is identified with specific characteristics, such as the existence of third-party affiliates or TPAs (also known as surrogacy agents) who liaise between clinics, surrogates, and couples. TPAs operate in Delhi and Mumbai in a big way, supporting clinics and hospitals. In Mumbai, unlike Delhi, surrogacy is marketed by large corporate TPAs. In Delhi, multi-speciality hospitals and stand-alone IVF clinics operate with TPAs. Deepa et al. suggest that in smaller towns such as Amritsar, IVF clinics operate through transnational networks dependent on transnational religious ties. For instance, the local gurdwara retains ties with other gurdwaras in countries such as Canada—having a considerable population of Sikh residents—prompting the travel of potential infertility clients to the IVF clinic through shared ties of religiosity.

In continuation, Deepa V. et al. suggest that in places such as Delhi, non-governmental organizations (NGOs) working in semi-urban areas recruit surrogates for the arrangement by linking their 'development' activities with nearby IVF clinics and surrogacy agencies. In Hyderabad, transnational networks help connect non-resident Indian (NRI) couples to affordable clinics and surrogates in India. The internet works particularly well in creating connections between the global and local through particular websites and blogs written by couples who had babies through surrogacy.

These forms of negotiations that local networks create to make transnational surrogacy networks viable are the unique aspects of transnational commercial surrogacy in India. The existence and proliferation of these networks is testimony that the complicated participation involved in arranging surrogacy is not only cultural, but may be a culture on its own.

Inhorn (2015) discusses the perils of reproductive travel in her monograph on South Asian couples travelling to Dubai to undergo fertility treatments. She finds the hardships involved in seeking fertility intervention in foreign countries as difficult and exhausting, as opposed to Speier's (2016) formulation that reproductive travel doubles up as a tourist/tourism enterprise with couples from the West benefitting from the cheaper services and relaxed environs of another country.

Most importantly, Inhorn (2015) discusses reproductive travel as part of 'global reproductive assemblages' that include travelling couples, gametes, and technologies across global reproductive hubs, such as India, and in her study, Dubai. Transnational commercial surrogacy in India occupies the space of a reproductive assemblage which refers to the power of global processes that create conflicts among local and transnational circuits of technology, people, finance, and markets. In that sense, the 'local', though important, is also constantly being subsumed by global processes. Despite the introduction of transnational commercial surrogacy in India—this book also focuses on the local within the global—the latter cannot be ignored in the formation and perpetuation of the former. This brings us back to the peculiarities of the engagement with commercial surrogacy and IVF in a setting that is fraught with varied conflicting processes. As this introduction proceeds, I look at the ways in which elements of the local have come to define transnational commercial surrogacy in India. This is purposely undertaken to move the focus away from its transnational–global character (not that that is not part of the discussion in this book), to engage with what the local entails in the procedure, processes, stories, and ideas that populate transnational commercial surrogacy in India.

Imagining Surrogacy in India

This book aims to understand and discuss the ways in which surrogacy is imagined in India, with its diverse portrayals in mythology, cinema, and popular culture. Here, one particular portrayal is deeply provocative, and is apt for introducing the issues and findings discussed in the book, some which include questions of parenthood, technology, commoditization, and the law.

Cash on Delivery

Two prominent news publications carried stories on surrogacy (in the year 2010). Both stories had the same title, 'Cash on Delivery', and carried source interviews of surrogates from the same clinic. However, the stance that the two stories took was very different from each other: while one raked up issues of ethics and the welfare of surrogates, the other saw this as an opportunity for many of the surrogates to change their life and gain financial independence.

These reports became the benchmark for most newspapers to use the 'industry' tag as a peg to look at how the commercial surrogacy industry in India was becoming a hotbed for an unregulated, thriving economy in reproductive labour. Many of them tagged India as a 'growth industry' and as the 'surrogacy hotspot'. Partly, the aim of such features was to highlight the growth of the reproductive tourism industry in India with the help of affordable medical care, and even cheaper surrogate services. To facilitate the growth of the industry, agents and marketing personnel of the IVF clinics began to advertise their services. In a section popularly known as the 'advertorial'—which was carried by many news magazines in the form of sponsored news items—a section on medical tourism appeared with a piece on

14

'Reproductive tourism—A reality of our times'. Write-ups like these (often contributed by IVF specialists) are a common feature and may act as votaries of the 'need for reproductive tourism', and at the same time advertise new technological innovations in the field of infertility treatment. The support of poor women through the burgeoning surrogacy industry became the prevalent motif for many IVF specialists who were actively pushing for legislation and government support for reproductive tourism. In the efforts at garnering support, mythology, films, and celebrities became part of the collective imagination surrounding commercial surrogacy in India.

Mythic Resonance

Surrogacy as a practice and idea has its roots in mythology and in contemporary discourses surrounding it. Simply put, when a woman agrees to participate in an arrangement that requires her to carry a pregnancy for a couple who seeks a child and are unable to have one, she is known as the surrogate. A critical part of this arrangement is the surrogate's relinquishment of the child in exchange for reimbursement. However, this definition fulfils only the basic contours of what surrogacy means; its actual permutations and combinations are far more complicated.

In mythology, both within Hinduism and Christianity, surrogacy involved sexual relationships between the man who would be the father and the surrogate. In the book of Genesis—in the Bible—the Egyptian maid to Abraham and Sarah, Hagar, is asked to bear a child for Abraham due to Sarah's infertility. Hagar begets Ishmael who goes on to become an important figure in the Semitic faiths. Known as traditional surrogacy, this practice involves sexual relationships between the surrogate and the father-to-be. Such an arrangement is not necessarily extinct, but may be contracted in secret—fearing social stigma. Contemporary technological interventions have created an important route to the ways in which surrogacy is conceptualized. Thus, current manifestations of surrogacy involve technology and different forms of participation that lead to the birth of a child. The myth of the birth of the Hindu god Krishna has been channelled by executives from the ICMR to make sense of gestational surrogacy in contemporary India. Legitimacy is sought through the constant resurrection of the Hindu myth of Krishna.

Elements of gestational and genetic surrogacy are interwoven with the fantastical in the myth of Krishna and his brother Balaram—both considered to be avatars of God Vishnu. According to the myth, Vishnu is asked to come to earth to relieve her of the burdens of man's evil ways. He makes way for his entry to earth in a new avatar. Here the evil incarnate is Kamsa. Each child born to Devki and Vasudev are preordained to die at the hands of Devki's brother, Kamsa, the evil ruler of Mithila—who does this to avert his prophesied death at the hands of one of Devki's children. As per the prophecy, the seventh child is ordained to kill Kamsa to end his evil ways, but in the process, Kamsa decides to kill all the children Devki gives birth to. Vasudev, Devki's husband convinces Kamsa to spare her life in return for each of the children she will bear. Kamsa imprisons Devki and Vasudev in anticipation of the birth of future children, each of whom he intends to kill. The first six babies born to Devki are killed by Kamsa by throwing the newborns against a stone. The seventh and eighth embryos become the important nodes of the birth of divinity. The seventh embryo, in the form of Balarama or Samskarasana, the brother of Krishna, suffers a miscarriage in Devki's womb, only to be miraculously transported into Vasudev's second wife, Rohini's, womb. Kamsa is told that the seventh birth was a miscarriage. The eighth birth is miraculous, heralding the birth of Krishna through the transposition of the baby Krishna with a goddess. While Devki gives birth to Krishna, a baby girl is born to a cowherd's wife, Yashoda. Through divine intervention (the opening of the gates of the palace prison, the parting of the river, the covering of

17

the baby in the basket by *sheshnag*, the celestial serpent), Vasudev secretly transports the newborn Krishna into Yashoda's cradle. Yashoda's baby girl is then taken to Devki, who pleads with Kamsa to spare her life, as a girl could do him no harm. Kamsa refuses to comply and dashes the baby on a stone, only to be rebuffed by the manifestation of the goddess who warns of his impending death at the hands of Krishna, who still lives.

In Pande's (2014) study of surrogates and surrogacy in India, the Krishna myth is invoked towards different ends by the surrogate, the clinician, and the surrogacy agent. The myth is evoked to justify commercial surrogate work, to train and indoctrinate surrogates into believing that they are carrying out god's work, and to justify one's role as god's messenger. Interestingly, at some point the Krishna myth morphs into the idea of 'surro-*dev*' a mythic conception of surrogacy as god himself—represented often through the imagery of the clinician. Materiality in this sense operates through a construction of divinity that is utilitarian and yet removed from worldly desires. A paradox indeed.

The Krishna myth comes to occupy an important counter narrative to the largely negative reports on commercial surrogacy that position it as a form of exploitative practice. It is meant to help create alternative discourses emerging from within the medical community in seeking to legalize surrogacy. This includes restricting access to certain constituencies who will understand and uphold its mythic underpinnings—such as NRIs who form a bulk of those commissioning surrogacy arrangements in India. Pandering to the Indian diaspora means feeding the traditional mythic India to them which is uncolonized and pristine in its birth myths. In that sense a refashioning of the self for NRIs would mean seeking to contract a surrogacy back home than anywhere else. It is an opportunity for them to gain access and draw from a culture and practices that are built in a glorious Hindu past, where the womb or *garbha* is so pure that it holds the divine itself. There cannot be a better advertisement for commercial surrogacy in India.

Filming the Surrogate Story

In popular Indian culture, surrogacy has come to be associated with the 2001 Hindi language film *Chori Chori Chupke Chupke* (Silently and Secretly), starring Bollywood superstar Salman Khan in the lead role. The film shows a prostitute being hired by an infertile couple in secret to birth their child. The prostitute is paid to have sex with the father-to-be and carry the child until she delivers it and relinquishes it to the adoptive mother. The plot of the film pre-empts the existence of IVF and involves traditional surrogacy, where the surrogate is also the genetic mother of the baby. In popular imagination, surrogacy is linked to this film, even though the plot is similar to a 1981 film called *Doosri Dulhan* (The Second Bride), where Shabana Azmi plays the role of the prostitute-surrogate.

The extension of the surrogate to the prostitute in both the films underlies the need for sexual relations to induce a pregnancy. The plots also identify the prostitute as the most eligible candidate for surrogacy, articulating fears of the shared links of surrogacy with sex work. Stigma and secrecy form a major part of the plot in the two films, as does the fear of intimacy between the intended father and the surrogate. Both the films have the intended parents contract the pregnancy with the prostitute in secret, after which she is whisked away to a distant location to hide the sexual act and the ensuing pregnancy. In *Chori Chori Chupke Chupke*, the intended parents (played by Salman Khan and Rani Mukherjee) create a parallel narrative for the intended father's extended family, where the pregnant surrogate is positioned as a friend's wife, and the intended mother creates a fake pregnancy. Such subterfuge marks the way in which surrogacy is perceived in the popular imagination—as a secret enterprise, always undertaken with linkages to paid sex work.

The narrative changed exponentially with the 2002 film *Filhaal*, whose plot involved a close friend volunteering to carry an IVF pregnancy for her infertile best friend. The film was not successful but introduced the idea of technological intervention to conceive. It also brought in the idea of a surrogate who was a close confidant and not a sex worker. This shift was important to create a change in the traditional association between surrogacy and sex work. It signalled the emergence of gestational labour that involved asexual reproduction. Yet, the intimacy emerging from the act of gestation itself could not be discounted. Thus, the anxieties and jealousy of close ties between the pregnant best friend and her husband unsettle the adoptive mother—leading to a break in their friendship.

The marital dyad—and the threat that surrogacy poses to it—continues to be a real challenge, despite the asexual mode of reproduction. In films such as *Doosri Dulhan*, *Chori Chori Chupke Chupke*, and *Filhaal*, this tension is exacerbated due to the sexual relations that the intended father and prostitute-surrogate share in the first two films, and the suggested intimacy, despite IVF, in the third film. In Pande's (2014) study of how surrogates find meaning in their pregnancy, the surrogate pregnancy is structured to keep out the men. Thus, the genetic father is not allowed to/ chooses not to meet the surrogate to avoid the stigma of unintended intimacy, even though the pregnancy is artificial. And the surrogate's husband stays away from the pregnancy as sex between him and the surrogate is forbidden for the period of nine months. In my ethnography (Majumdar 2017), the surrogate husband has to take responsibility of the surrogate pregnancy as a co-signatory to the surrogacy contract and cannot be distant anymore.

The relationship between the adoptive mother and the surrogate is tense and, yet, tender. The former is deeply invested in the pregnancy, despite reservations and the fear of losing her unborn child and husband. Ragone (1994) conducted one of the first pioneering studies of commercial surrogacy in the USA, titled *Conception from the Heart*, and spoke of the ambiguities that threaten the relationship between the adoptive mother-to-be and the surrogate. In her study, conducted in the late 1980s, the surrogates were genetic—contributing their eggs and uterus to the pregnancy. This meant that the separation between the egg donor and the surrogate, which is part of the gestational arrangement, was not possible then. This, effectively, made the surrogate the 'mother', with no contribution from the adoptive mother, while the sperm came from the intended father. The sexual and intimate undertones of such a relationship, even though it was enacted through artificial insemination, made the entire arrangement difficult for the adoptive mother to adjust to. The surrogates in Ragone's (1996) study had to perform elaborate rituals and put in immense effort to convince the adoptive mother of her ownership of the pregnancy. This meant a stronger bond between the surrogate and the adoptive mother, and a sustained, deliberate distance between the intended father and the surrogate.

The prostitute-surrogate is even more complex, despite the one-dimensional portrayal in *Doosri Dulhan* and *Chori Chori Chupke Chupke* of a woman who is greedy, and ready to step in as wife and mother in the threatened marital dyad once she herself is pregnant. In both the films, the prostitutes—Shabana Azmi as Chanda in *Doosri Dulhan* and Preity Zinta as Madhubala in *Chori Chori Chupke Chupke*—invoke caricatures but also point towards the unpleasantness of relinquishing a child, or more importantly, not wanting a child. They represent the ambiguities within motherhood, which are eulogized in cinematic portrayals as suffering and sacrifice. Only as prostitutes—already 'fallen women'—can Chanda and Madhubala get away with bearing and relinquishing their children. They are despised, but forgiven—it is their 'nature'. But when the prostitute-surrogate seeks legitimacy through marriage with the intended father and by running away with the child, she is brought back to the institutionalized understanding of her place in society. Both the films end with Chanda and Madhubala as 'rescued'—they do not go back to prostitution. Motherhood has changed them: Chanda becomes a *jogin* or renunciate and Madhubala goes away to a foreign country. Both transformations signal an escape from their past, seeking changes that either divorce them from their home and culture, or which reject a sexual life and the household.

In *Filhaal*, too, where the surrogate (played by Sushmita Sen) fulfils the altruistic act of helping her friend (played by Tabu) by having her child, the redemption for an act of 'madness' (becoming pregnant outside of marriage) is through domesticity with her long-time beau. The madness of her decision to have a child as an unmarried woman, and then relinquishing it, marks the friend-surrogate in *Filhaal* in aberrant terms—just like the prostitute-surrogates in the other two films. Thus, Sia, the friend-surrogate is shown as overtly ambitious and someone who shuns domesticity—in many ways, almost masculine. In an earlier psychological study of the motivations of surrogates, Parker (1983) finds women who seek to be surrogates as aberrant and abnormal, in their desire to be pregnant, and eventually give up the child they carry. In her book, *Motherhood and Choice: Uncommon Mothers, Childfree Women*, Nandy (2017) finds parallels between single mothers, childfree women, and surrogates as those who are questioning the dominant understanding of women and motherhood. Similarly, in all three films discussed above, the surrogate—though necessary to fulfil another woman's role as mother and wife—is nonetheless not the norm. She is destabilizing and, therefore, cannot be praised or made into a standard. In many ways the surrogate cannot be made the conventional Indian heroine—she must be represented as 'abnormal'.

Celebrity Culture

If Bollywood films have represented surrogacy in interesting ways, film stars and the surrounding celebrity culture have not been different either. Since Bollywood actor Aamir Khan announced the birth of his child through surrogacy in 2011, many other stars and actors have followed suit, leading to the emergence of commercial surrogacy in India from a different perspective. The Aamir Khan–Kiran Rao case marks some interesting changes in the way surrogacy was being perceived vis-à-vis the infertile couple. For one, the focus was understandably on the celebrity couple and their newborn; but there was an obliteration of the role of the surrogate. In fact, unlike similar earlier stories, the use of the term 'IVF-surrogacy', instead of commercial surrogacy, signalled a move away from the acknowledgement of the surrogate's role in the birth of the child. The focus was on the adoptive mother—Kiran Rao. This had a lot to do with the way the adoptive mother herself exhibited a strong and independent personality. This was evident in the report that Aamir Khan had left the decision of naming the child to his wife, leading to the name Azad Rao Khan—containing both parents' surnames—a practice that is not common in patriarchal India. Reports stated that Kiran had suffered a miscarriage earlier on, which had led to complications in having children. Thus, the couple had to take the help of fertility specialist, Dr Firuza Parikh, to have their son through a surrogate in a Mumbai hospital.

The press lauded the couple for their outspokenness and called Aamir the 'poster boy' for the surrogacy industry; and such 'praise' was not misplaced for, finally, as many IVF specialists testified, a heterosexual couple had openly come out in support and endorsement of the use of a surrogate to have a child. This also started the trend for other Bollywood celebrities to choose to have children through surrogacy and be open about it. So, Shahrukh Khan, Karan Johar, and Tusshar Kapoor, proudly announced the birth of their children through IVF-surrogacy and received ample media attention.

The impact of this celebrity culture surrounding IVF-surrogacy was particularly important in promoting what Bharadwaj (2000) calls the 'routinization' of infertility treatment and IVF. To move away from its stigmatizing nature that makes many infertile couples seek secrecy during treatment, celebrity endorsements of IVF-surrogacy has meant more publicity and a form of 'openness' about treating infertility and contracting surrogacy, which was absent earlier. But celebrity endorsements have also hidden and exacerbated other conversations regarding commercial surrogacy in India.

Absence of the Mother

Each of the births—of Aamir Khan's son, Shahrukh Khan's son, Tusshar Kapoor's son, and Karan Johar's twins—have been about the celebrities and very little about the women who have helped birth them. Kiran Rao is prominently part of the media representations of the birth of Aamir Khan's son, and the presumption is that she may be the genetic mother of the baby—having given her eggs to the surrogate pregnancy. But as mentioned in the beginning of this chapter, the surrogate remains in the background, almost shrouded in invisibility and secrecy. Such a representation is repeated across the stories of each of the other celebrity-babies' births. None of the actors mention their egg donors or surrogates; and in case of Shahrukh Khan there is also an absence of his wife, Gauri Khan, in the media narratives. The reference

27

to IVF-surrogacy positions the birth of the children as 'miraculous' and emerging from technology: the surrogate is an afterthought, almost an appendage. None of the celebrities speak of the surrogate, but they all thank their infertility specialists/doctors. This purported absence of the surrogate is part of how IVF-surrogacy positions itself, wherein the surrogate is meant to be invisible. Her identity has to be kept a secret due to the intimate nature of the pregnancy and the ways in which she threatens the genetic link that the couple/single parent shares with the child. That Indian surrogates belong largely to a lower socio-economic category also means that there is much squeamishness to acknowledge their contribution.

Focus on the Single Father

IVF-surrogacy has become the route to parenthood for many male celebrities in Bollywood who are single and seek children without entering into conventional relationships, such as marriage. In many ways the choice of surrogacy amongst celebrities such as Tusshar Kapoor and Karan Johar signals not only the rejection of heterosexual conjugality, but also of adoption. Now, children can be genetically linked to the single man seeking fatherhood, especially considering Indian laws that prohibit single men from adopting girl children.

The attention that single fatherhood through IVF-surrogacy has generated has meant that otherwise taboo conversations regarding sexuality, families, and marriage have become part of the subtext of these media narratives. Yet, interestingly, none of the single fathers themselves have admitted to these tradition-bending practices with much fervour, instead going back to the conventional family paradigm of descent and kinship to give legitimacy to their newborn children. Akin to the missing surrogate in other celebrity surrogacy births, all the celebrity single fathers go back to endorsing and upholding the traditional familial structure, while subtly subverting it by having children through surrogacy.

The tacit promotion and normalization of IVF-surrogacy through the preponderance of online celebrity cultures means that there is very little conversation on the ways in which the arrangement facilitates the birth of children. This includes the absence of conversations regarding homosexuality and its 'illegality'[1] in India, or the difficult legal landscape that makes adoption

---

[1] As of 2018, the Supreme Court of India has removed the offensive Indian Penal Code Section 377 that criminalized certain sexual acts including homosexuality, signalling new changes in how law views homosexuality and homosexual relations in India.

a 'non-option', as Bharadwaj (2003) calls it. Most importantly, the popularity of IVF-surrogacy promotes a pronatalist, genetic culture that is embedded in the importance of patriarchal descent through men and the absence or ignorance of the gestational role that women play in birthing children. This is discussed further in Chapter 4.

IVF-surrogacy in contemporary India has, unfortunately, become a celebrity endorsement industry, dominated by images of familial togetherness and perfect cherubic babies. It ignores the poor women who form an important part of the arrangement, the men and women who suffer silently through infertility due to lack of financial support to contract a surrogacy arrangement, and those children who are languishing in orphanages.

★★★

Many of the arguments discussed in this book draw from recent outstanding research work conducted on transnational surrogacy. India has been at the centre of all the conversations on transnational surrogacy, primarily because it has within it all the structural conditions that fuel the desire for commercial gestates. One of the most important prerequisites for gestational surrogacy is a thriving state-of-the-art medical industry that is largely run by private hospitals and conglomerates. In India, today, the infertility medicine industry operates primarily in the private sector. Public, institutionalized health care is not available for infertility treatment and cure. However, other forms of reproductive technologies, primarily dealing with preventing conception, are largely state-supported. Within such a setting, infertility medicine comes to occupy the terrain of what is now being called reproductive tourism. Besides figures that identify this as a fast-growing segment within the larger medical tourism industry, commercial surrogacy remained the primary locus of the reproductive tourism industry for a long time. Of late, the commercial gestational surrogacy industry has grabbed the most eyeballs within reproductive tourism. Thus, we are now beginning to see the rise of a new form of medical engagement with an overseas clientele. For long, commercial surrogacy was embraced as a positive element of transnational ties, laying claim to vast figures of trade as predicted by the Confederation of Indian Industries (CII) and McKinsey (CII–McKinsey 2002). But, the human angle, that of the Indian surrogate, continued to add to its progress and status.

With respect to the chapters that follow, this short introduction aims to bring to you some of the important debates that have come to mark commercial surrogacy arrangements in India. Its transnational nature, which is now under scrutiny, has been the subject of extensive and detailed ethnographies (a list has been provided at the end of this book), but here is a starting point in order to understand the different sets of participants within the arrangement. The key to comprehending the ways in which commercial surrogacy has operated in India is through the participants' perspective.

Before embarking on a detailed discussion, following are some terms which you need to remember when reading the text.

Intended Parents/Commissioning Couples   These are terms used interchangeably throughout the text to refer to couples who commission, and are part of, a surrogacy arrangement. They are identified as heterosexual and suffering from varied levels of infertility, but may also include homosexual men and women who seek to have biological progeny through this arrangement.

Adoptive Mothers   This is used to refer to women who commission a surrogacy arrangement as 'adoptive mothers', in keeping with Ragone's (1996) conceptualization.

It is also important to note here that the intended parent/commissioning couple undertake what Inhorn

(2015) has referred to as 'reprotravel' across borders to fulfil their desire to have children. Reprotravellers may not necessarily be couples travelling for international adoption, but they certainly include couples— heterosexual and homosexual—seeking ARTs and surrogacy. It is in this vein that other terms have surfaced to describe the extraordinary journeys that couples take to have children across the world. Because they seek services outside their home countries—for varied reasons such as expenses, lack of availability of technology and surrogates, legal prohibitions, and/ or stigma—many of these reprotravellers are also 'reproductive exiles' (Inhorn 2015). As mentioned earlier in the chapter, the reproductive exiles in Inhorn's study undergo social and financial struggles to access IVF and surrogacy outside their countries. However, they do so because many of those travelling from the Global North to the Global South have at their disposal more options in the transnational reproductive 'marketplace'. Krolokke and Pant (2012) call couples travelling for reproductive services 'repropreneurs'—those who make informed decisions about available options in the neoliberal reproductive tourism industry. In that sense, for Krolokke and Pant, couples who are 'repropreneurs' have greater control over their reproductive features, unlike the reproductive exiles.

Commercial/Gestational Surrogate This refers to the woman who volunteers to participate in the commercial surrogacy arrangement as a gestational surrogate. The focus on the gestational role means that Indian women who enter the surrogacy arrangement as surrogates are only allowed to participate as carriers of the artificially fertilized foetus. In other special cases, the surrogate is identified accordingly. Here, I purposely move away from attaching 'mother' to surrogate as it comes with its own set of politics and problems which will be discussed in the chapters to come.

IVF Specialist/ART Clinic This refers to the IVF doctor who facilitates the technology and its use, within the space of the ARTs or IVF clinic. The specialist and the clinic are interchangeable because the former cannot work outside the ambit of the latter. They are deeply intertwined by the demands of the surrogacy technology and the ways in which it is structured.

Surrogacy Agents/TPAs (Third-Party Affiliates) These are the primary facilitators in the surrogacy arrangement in India. They recruit surrogates, connect clinics with surrogates and couples, and organize the entire arrangement for couples, including hiring legal help. The transnational scope of the arrangement was

34

facilitated by surrogacy agents, who created a massive demand for surrogacy services in India amongst foreign couples. The 'package deals' that provided IVF–surrogacy to foreign couples at competitive rates and included tourism packages as well were an important part of the surrogacy agents' work.

Many of the terms discussed above are not watertight in their meanings and definitions. Invoking Inhorn's (2015) discussion on the 'reprolexicon', the lexicon created by me in the earlier paragraphs is debated upon and dissected as this book develops. Inhorn's reprolexicon, in turn, aims to engage with theoretical ideas in circulation in anthropology with emerging research on reproductive travel. Inhorn introduces new terminology that engages with the conflicts and processes that exist within reproductive travel. This includes seeking answers from those who are part of the transnational circuits of reproductive travel, such as couples, surrogates, and donors, besides doctors and agents.

As mentioned in this introduction, each of the chapters in this book deals with a particular perspective of transnational commercial gestational surrogacy arrangement (TCGSA) from the vantage point of the participants identified above. Chapters 2 and 5 deal specifically with elements of the commercial surrogacy arrangement such as the law and the technology. Chapters 3 and 4 are dedicated to the surrogate and the couple who form the most important link in the arrangement.

The aim of the book is to provide a bird's-eye view of commercial gestational surrogacy in India by provoking conversations and debates regarding the feasibility and preponderance of values attached to the practice of birthing a child 'artificially'.

2

The Technology

How In Vitro Fertilization Works in Commercial Surrogacy

IVF is part of a large body of ARTs, including intracystoplasmic injection (ICSI) and IUI among others. ARTs in turn are part of new reproductive technologies (NRTs) that include technologies for termination and prevention of pregnancies as well. Conservative estimates places the number of ART clinics at 3,000, according to the ICMR; the Indian Society of Assisted Reproduction (ISAR) membership has reportedly grown from 184 (in 1997) to 600 (in 2005). Making latest statistics on IVF clinics available remain an uphill task as many clinics do not register themselves.

The coming in of IVF, and later other ARTs, has been a godsend for many. The popularity of ARTs can also be placed within a culture that privileges fertility as sacrosanct. The Indian Council of Medical Research's Draft ARTs Bill (ICMR 2010: 1) begins on an ominous note: 'In India infertility widely carried with it a social stigma. In the Indian social context specially, children are also a kind of old-age insurance.'

The first test-tube baby in India was born in the 1970s, but the birth led to the untimely demise of its creator due to the largely negative reactions he received from the scientific community. Bharadwaj (2002) studies the politics of counter-claims made in seeking research credibility in the development of IVF in India, which led to the suicide of Dr Subhas Mukherjee in 1978 due to a lack of support from the medical community for the development of the first test-tube baby in India.

Cut to the 1980s and the birth of the second test-tube baby. The large-scale press coverage it received led to the routinization of IVF technology. According to Bharadwaj (2016), shifting the focus on technology meant generating interest in the way that ARTs came to occupy a place of its own within gynaecology departments. The boom in infertility treatments have become more and more pronounced over the last decade, ever since the rise of infertility as a lifestyle disease. Newspaper reports and discussion pieces are increasingly obsessing about why urban India is beginning to 'suffer' from childlessness.

Despite the prohibition against recruitment advertisements for donors and/or surrogates, ART clinics often advertise their technology and success rates in mainstream newspapers and through online websites in the form of overt self-advertising, which also fulfils the need to recruit surreptitiously. This has now become an essential part of the burgeoning new medical tourism industry in India, which commands impressive revenue figures. For instance, as per media reports, an IVF cycle in India costs approximately US $2,000 in comparison to the US $20,000 per cycle in the USA, or the £7,000 per cycle in the United Kingdom (UK). (These costs have changed considerably and may vary from region to region.) The affordable pricing is a big draw for medical tourists across the globe with an estimated growth of four billion US dollars for the medical tourism industry in India by 2012. The National Health Bill 2009, with the help of CII forecasts, legalizes medical tourism and reduces the role of the state in the availability of free medical care, introducing private involvement in a big way.

The medical tourism industry caters to most major health services, including organ transplantation, intensive surgeries, and intensive care.

The reproductive tourism industry has been thriving off the provision of cost-effective commercial surrogacy packages. In 2011, newspaper reports suggested that US $12,000–28,000 could fund a decent surrogacy arrangement, inclusive of the surrogate's fees, IVF/ICSI costs, and other additional expenses, such as hotel stay and visa fees. The bulk of the earnings go to the IVF clinics which administer the treatment and hire the anonymous donor and the surrogate. The surrogates receive only a fraction of this cost.

Alarmed at the rising involvement of IVF specialists in the surrogacy 'business', the ICMR began to contemplate regulating the sourcing and recruitment of surrogates via IVF clinics. In their 2010 bill, ICMR recommended setting up 'ART Banks', which would monitor recruitment and liaison with clinics to facilitate a better commercial surrogacy arrangement, while at the same time keeping copious records of each arrangement that was commissioned. The primary role envisaged for these ART Banks was as record keepers who would keep a database of surrogates and donors as well as intended parents who have commissioned a surrogacy arrangement.

Many such ART Banks began to emerge in the guise of surrogacy agencies, and TPAs, who began to recruit surrogates and egg donors for commercial surrogacy arrangements.

Modes of Recruitment

The medicalization of commercial gestational surrogacy is dependent on the ready 'availability' of the surrogate and anonymous donors (wherever required). However, not many women are willing to participate in the surrogacy arrangement, skewing the relationship between the demand for and supply of surrogates. This means that clinics have to engage in elaborate processes by which they can recruit surrogates. In the ICMR Draft Bill 2010, provisions for ART Banks were made to facilitate easier access to surrogates and donors, thereby restricting the role of the IVF clinic to providing only the treatment. These ART Banks will operate in conjunction with ART clinics to provide surrogates and anonymous donors. The clinics are supposed to source gamete donors from the ART Banks as well as follow certain standard ethical guidelines laid down by the ICMR including prohibition against sex determination of foetus, regulation of sale and research of gametes and embryos, obtaining informed consent from all participants, and maintaining a record of all donor gametes—embryos used as well as surrogacy arrangements undertaken. This was an important and necessary intervention, considering how IVF clinics were doubling up as recruiters and compromising on their primary responsibility of administering the

41

ART–IVF treatment. The suggestion to form ART Banks also came due to the emerging recruiters and surrogacy agencies, who fulfilled the demand from clinics and couples for surrogates and egg donors. In a tiered set-up, as discussed by Nadimpally and Majumdar (2017) in their article on 'agent-facilitators' in the commercial surrogacy arrangement, the recruitment followed spatial patterns of linking major multinational agencies with local neighbourhood recruiters.

There are primarily two different types of recruiters/ agents. The first is the neighbourhood agent who sources the surrogates and donors directly. In Deomampo's (2016) detailed description of one such agent–recruiter, she finds that the agent had once been a surrogate herself. After she completed her first surrogacy, the agent transitioned into becoming a recruiter. In the process she earned some money and now used her experience as a surrogate to inform, cajole, and recruit other women from her own and adjoining neighbourhoods to join the arrangement. Every new recruit fetched a considerable commission. Most such neighbourhood recruiters were found to be ex-surrogates and operated between clinics and agencies with great dexterity. According to Nadimpally and Majumdar (2017), many of them were men who would begin by introducing their wives into the arrangement. Neighbourhood, local recruiters operate mostly from lower income group slums and shanties in cities such as Mumbai and Delhi. They also doubled up as 'caretakers' during the surrogate pregnancy—administering medicines on behalf of the clinic and generally monitoring the surrogate's diets and habits. According to Sama's (2012) research, a culture of surveillance was perpetuated during the pregnancy, and this was particularly invasive for many of the women. For those surrogates who would opt to stay outside the hostel, in their homes, or in rented accommodation—the neighbourhood grocer would be asked to keep an eye on the diet of the surrogate based on her purchase of grocery items. Others such as Saravanan (2010) note that the recruitment of surrogates followed particular forms of eligibility criteria. In Mumbai, for instance, she found agencies and clinics actively seeking docile, submissive women who would not ask too many questions and cooperate throughout the arrangement. Any sign of 'aggression' or inquisitive behaviour immediately led to rejection as a potential surrogate.

The final sifting was done by agencies that operate as TPAs. Deepa V. et al. (2013) find TPAs with different and varying levels of financial investments. Multinational TPAs have agencies around the world and facilitate regular trips for intended parents and Caucasian egg donors to India. Many of them set up shop in India to cash in on the increasing demand for surrogates. There are also Indian agencies which were run as businesses, funded by pharmaceutical companies. But by its very definition, the TPA existed as a formal liaison that connected clinics, donors, surrogates, and intended parents.

TPAs would often aggressively sift through the women brought by the neighbourhood agents before including them in the roster to be used by clinics and intended parents. They would cater to requirements of caste, class, race, and religion if required, but were also sensitive to the appearance and social background of the potential surrogates as well as the intended parents. Thus, intended parents were usually provided with an extensive roster of egg donors, highlighting their educational background, appearances, and familial history. In case of surrogate mothers, such a roster may not always be made available. Often couples would go with the doctor's preference of the surrogate.

Such a marked difference in the process of choosing the surrogate and the egg donor corresponds to the ways in which agencies and doctors position them for couples. The egg donor is carefully sifted and handpicked by couples due to the idea that her genes will be the most important aspect of the to-be-born child's genetic make-up. On the other hand, the surrogate's gestational role is constantly focused upon, separating her from the foetus. The fleeting engagement with the egg donor—who may often remain anonymous—means that couples are encouraged to be more involved in choosing her than the surrogate. The surrogate, on the other hand, is far too close for comfort. Her appearance is not important, but her fertility is definitely important. For this, doctors and agencies remain important arbitrators. Vora (2013) finds the differential treatment meted out to surrogates as part of an elaborate set-up wherein her poverty is constantly part of the clinic's positioning of her choice and participation in the arrangement. Pande (2011) speaks of the kind of discomfort the physical proximity of the surrogate provokes amongst IPs, who are protected by clinics and agents through the elaborate geographical, cultural, and linguistic distance between them.

Most importantly, according to my study (Majumdar 2017), TPAs and local recruiters actively promote the sense that a surrogate pregnancy is distant for the surrogate and closer for the intended parents. This involved active distanciation by making the pregnancy itself seem 'artificial' for the surrogate so that she may not feel emotionally attached to it, thereby not making relinquishment a problem. Many surrogates still created linkages with the baby, the way Pande (2009) notes, by recognizing their 'labour' of gestation.

Risky Pregnancy

A significant part of the IVF-surrogacy process is focused on the nine months of the pregnancy. As an artificial biomedical intervention, there is not much research on the nature of the pregnancy and its health impact on the surrogate. Amongst the studies conducted on the health risks that surrogates face is a detailed analysis by Sama (2012) in their study on commercial gestational surrogacy in India. Sama's research findings chronicle the kind of risks that surrogates undergo during the pregnancy.

The study notes that the insistence on gestational surrogacy means that the intervention of IVF becomes mandatory. With this intervention comes deeply intrusive procedures that play havoc with the surrogate's reproductive health. Some of those procedures include repeated IVF cycles of introducing the embryo into the surrogate's uterus, primarily because procedures of embryo transfer (ET) may not always lead to a pregnancy. Each cycle is accompanied by preparing the uterus with hormones that include a strict regimen of movement and diet post ET. Similar procedures of artificially stimulating the ovary are followed amongst egg donors; one case in 2014, involving the death of an egg donor in a clinic in Delhi due to excessive bleeding after a procedure of extracting her eggs for a surrogacy, was linked to OHSS (ovarian hyperstimulation syndrome). In January 2014, twenty-six-year-old Yuma Sherpa died after a surgical procedure meant to extract her oocytes, for which she had earlier been injected with hormones to induce super ovulation to produce more eggs than the singular egg that is released in every menstrual cycle. The case was referred to the medical council for investigation for medical negligence and malpractice.

The surrogate does not necessarily have to go through over stimulation of her ovaries, but her uterus has to be prepared for the ET. This involves many invasive procedures and multiple risks to the surrogate which are often not discussed. A large part of the process is shrouded in secrecy and lack of information—especially regarding the medical interventions involved. It begins with the preliminary tests to check the surrogate's health—including blood tests, urine tests, and ultrasounds—to determine her obstetric history. Surrogates reportedly knew very little about these tests and were not informed about the same (Sama 2012).

This lack of information translated into vetting processes that distanced surrogates from the procedures undertaken and exposed them to disproportionate information about the process and their role in it. The medicalization of the surrogate pregnancy primarily involved the following three stages of risky health practices for the surrogates, according to the Sama (2012) study.

Pre-pregnancy

The overt focus on the separation of genes and gestate means that surrogates are valued (and de-valued) at different levels of the IVF process. Thus, sterilized women are preferred in the role of the gestational surrogate as it is presumed that the 'fear' of a genetic link, through the egg of the surrogate, is eradicated this way. Such thinking is reflected in the legal documents that the surrogate signs, which have very little or no information regarding the medical procedures that she will have to undertake. Her co-signatory, her husband, nearest male relative, or a relative from her husband's side makes her involvement in the arrangement even more precarious and devoid of any exercise of choice. Commissioning couples and the surrogate's husband take decisions regarding her body and the medical procedures involved, without her knowledge and express consent. As the Sama (2012) study suggests, most surrogates interviewed knew very little about the procedures they would be undergoing or had already undergone, but could clearly articulate who the pregnancy belonged to, genetically. This means that the surrogate goes through multiple cycles of ETs with repeated hormonal cycles, medication, and diet and movement control. The surrogate is never informed that the pregnancy may not happen in the first attempt and that IVF is not a foolproof technology. The multiple ETs become part of the process for her, and its transformation into a pregnancy is made the surrogate's responsibility. Thus, the rhetoric surrounding the surrogate's participation in the arrangement puts her not only in an unequal position vis-à-vis the technology, but also puts the onus of a faulty technology on her. Any miscarriage, which is a regular part of the IVF story, is blamed on the surrogate and her lack of care after the ET. Such blame is also placed on infertile women who undergo IVF procedures, placing their emotional and physical health in a precarious position.

Pregnancy

To circumvent the flawed IVF cycle, doctors often make multiple ETs, leading to multiple pregnancies. Many embryos may be introduced to ensure a single pregnancy. Again, the Sama study found that surrogates were not informed that they were being inseminated with multiple embryos, and would only find out once the pregnancy test would come back positive with more than one pregnancy. Multiple pregnancies were not always sought after by commissioning couples, leading to foetal reduction or abortion of unwanted foetus—another invasive procedure. An Irish couple reported feeling extreme regret when their clinic in Mumbai chose to abort one of the three foetuses that had been implanted into their Indian surrogate, resulting in multiple pregnancies. They did not have a choice in preventing the abortion as the clinic had a policy allowing only twin pregnancies.

This lack of choice meant that both couples and surrogates were subject to the clinic's decisions, irrespective of how they felt about the procedures. The surrogate's consent was never sought regarding any of the procedures, nor was she informed about the invasive and possibly harmful effects. This lack of choice or control over her pregnancy and body meant that the surrogate had no choice of opting out of the pregnancy. Abortion choices were not available to her, and in case of a miscarriage she was held responsible for having jeopardized the pregnancy. In the film *Can We See the Baby Bump, Please?* (produced by Sama and the Magic Lantern Foundation in 2012), one of the surrogates interviewed recounts her ordeal at the IVF clinic after a miscarriage. After bleeding heavily due to the miscarriage, she is prematurely discharged with some medication, despite not having recovered fully.

When the surrogate goes back to receive some of the compensation she was promised for her pregnancy, she is summarily dismissed and blamed for the miscarriage and sent away without any payment.

It is important to understand that the compensation given to the surrogate follows different rules in different clinics and agencies; but by and large it is divided up into dietary payments for the nine months, pre-pregnancy incentives, and post delivery payment. Often, surrogates have reported getting some money on getting pregnant. However, if there is a miscarriage, they do not get any money at all. In such a scenario, pregnancy and birthing follow a system of incentives.

Post Pregnancy

In keeping with an incentivized system, the Sama (2012) study finds that the frequency of caesarean deliveries—in case of surrogate pregnancies—was explained in terms of the safety of the child and a safe delivery, but was also insidiously linked to the availability and convenience of the foreign couple travelling to India for the birth of the baby. While a caesarean delivery benefits the clinic/hospital as it adds to the already burgeoning bill, it jeopardizes the surrogate's health through post delivery excessive bleeding and abdominal pain.

Surrogates were given medication to suppress the post delivery pain as well as lactation. In the Sama research, surrogates were reportedly not allowed to breastfeed after the delivery, based on ideas of emotional intimacy developing through the act of lactation between the surrogate and the newborn. However, the pills given to suppress lactation had various side effects, including nausea, dizziness, and hair loss. The possibility of breast engorgement was also reported in cases of suppressed lactation amongst surrogates. Based on the fear of the surrogate's bond with the newborn—and the associated anxieties regarding her relinquishing the child—many intended parents tacitly agreed to the sudden break of the child from the surrogate. At the same time, post delivery care for the surrogate after the hormonal invasions and caesarean sections was minimal. Sama reports that most of the interviewed surrogates got only sporadic medical care after the delivery of the child. The distance between surrogates and the commissioning couple meant that she was all but forgotten, post the delivery of the child. This form of marked negligence then leads to the surrogate entering a vicious cycle of multiple surrogate pregnancies to offset the kind of compensation she receives.

★★★

The IVF culture in India forms an important part of the commercial gestational surrogacy arrangement. Within such a culture, the health risks that technology and its unregulated practise poses to the surrogate's body is not taken into consideration. Chatterjee and Wheelan (2017)—of the Boston Women's Collective that brought out the iconic book *Our Bodies, Ourselves*— find certain problematic and outstanding elements of transnational commercial surrogacy across the world as downplaying the health hazards the surrogate is subject to.

This is part of a larger rhetoric that positions the surrogacy arrangement through the use of IVF as a 'delivery' system where the child is the 'product' and 'choice' is something that only the commissioning couple can exercise. The surrogate is a service provider who is made to believe that she is expendable, even though she is an important part of the commercial surrogacy arrangement, as the next chapter will show.

3

The Surrogate 'Mother'
Contractual Labour as Selfless Mothers

Hum uski kouk kiraye pe le lenge.
Aisa kaun aurat karegi?!
Jise paise ka lalach ho. Kyun, jab ek aurat paise ke liye
apne aap ko bech sakti hai, woh ek saal ke liye bhi bik
sakti hai.

[We will rent her womb.
What kind of woman would be ready to do that?!
A woman who has greed for money. Why, if a
woman can sell herself for money–, then she will
certainly be willing to be bought for a year.]
(*Doosri Dulhan*, 1982)

This is how the character of Renu sets the tone for
hiring a prostitute to become a surrogate mother to
her and her husband, Anil's child in *Doosri Dulhan*. She

profiles the prospective surrogate mother as someone who will be willing to sell herself and her body to carry another's child for money. Anil zeroes in on the prostitute Chanda in a scene where he sees her haggling with a customer for a small amount. Chanda further proves her suitability by saying that she hates the idea of motherhood and is finally convinced to carry the child, in exchange for a large amount of money.

In the 1980s, with the looming yet unrecognized existence of IVF, the idea of a woman renting out her womb was close to the idea of renting out her body. In the film *Doosri Dulhan*, the controversial status of the unacknowledged first Indian test-tube baby is mentioned in a slightly derisive tone. According to actress Shabana Azmi, who played the role of the prostitute–surrogate Chanda, the film was way ahead of its time. In an interview, Azmi mentioned how she researched for the role of a prostitute rather than that of a surrogate as it was unheard of in India when the film came out in 1982. To carry someone's child meant having sexual relations with the husband. That this involved a transaction of money and morals meant that only the 'fallen' woman could fulfil such an act.

The dramatic media representation of commercial gestational surrogacy in India is obsessed with its commercial side. The multi-layered representation of the surrogacy arrangement juggles with the image of the surrogate, the contract, and the technology that makes it possible. In this chapter, I look at the ways in which the idea of commerce and commodities is intrinsically connected to the notion of labour and motherhood within commercial surrogacy in India.

Surrogacy has been seen as an acute form of the commoditization of reproduction wherein, thanks to the intervention of NRTs, the foetus tends to be distanced from the pregnant woman. This gives rise to notions of separateness and the foetus is given a status that is higher than that of the living woman carrying it. At the same time, the idea of motherhood as an indissoluble status, marked by intense social values and morals, is very much part of the discourse.

Thus, the representation of the surrogate as mother and woman are constantly conflicted within popular representations. In media representations of Indian surrogates, they are still portrayed as women who agree to become pregnant for money because they are impoverished and need support for their own children.

The fascination with which we treat the surrogate means that she continues to be the most important element in the policy, for academics, and in the media discourse on surrogacy. But what is it about the surrogate that fascinates us so much? Is it the combination of her desire to birth and relinquish or our own idealized notions of being and becoming mothers that prejudices us towards her? Over the next few sections we will analyse how and why motherhood comes to be imagined and remanufactured within commercial surrogacy, and what impact it has on the Indian surrogate.

Contracting Motherhood

As per figures gathered in New Delhi during my fieldwork between 2011 and 2013, a surrogacy 'agreement' would cost anything between INR 4–4.5 lakh (1 lakh = 100,000) for the entire transaction, including the surrogate's fee of INR 2.5 lakh, and an additional INR 1 lakh for her diet and comfort over the gestation period of nine months. The remaining INR 50,000 go to the medical practitioner who arranged for the transaction. Contrary to newspaper reportage, couples seeking surrogacy services would pay approximately INR 10–15 lakhs, which is much less when compared to INR 25–35 lakh in the USA for the same services.

However, these costs are variable not only internationally, but differ within India as well. Newspaper reports in 2010–11 quoted similar amounts in contracting a surrogacy arrangement.

When the Law Commission identifies 'wombs on rent' as potential dollars, we begin to think of the ways in which commercialization is the driving force of the surrogacy arrangement in India. In merely a few words, the womb is separated from the woman and positioned as a potential earner.

The commodification of the arrangement includes different kinds of medical and social expectations from the surrogate. A surrogate should ideally be 'healthy', married, and have at least one child of her own. (There are cases where an unmarried woman may become a surrogate. This category excludes widows and divorced women, though they too volunteer to be surrogates.) For a mere INR 1–3.5 lakh, couples can also choose a surrogate of a particular determination (religious or caste affiliation) and with no 'vices' such as smoking or drinking. Post selection the surrogate must undergo extensive medical tests, beginning with endoscopy, the insemination of the eggs, and so on, culminating into a pregnancy. In most cases the eggs are not that of the surrogate—they may have been donated by the woman who has hired the surrogate and is the intended mother, or may belong to an anonymous donor. As mentioned earlier, gestational surrogacy is the only legally allowed form of surrogacy in India.

One of the reasons why gestational surrogacy is encouraged over genetic surrogacy is because of the belief that there would be no genetic link between the surrogate and the foetus, and also a lack of emotional connect between them. According to studies, Indian surrogates are trained to consider themselves as rooms for rent; this is to reduce their attachment to the child and give in to their representation of being incubators. The compensation given to the surrogates is meant to cover not only the cost of the labour, but also to ensure that the contract is carried through so that, at the end of the deal, the surrogate gives up the baby.

Relinquishment of the child informs the tone and tenor of the contract. The surrogacy contract is a document that has within it many of the important elements of the overwhelming commercialization of the surrogacy arrangement in India. But most importantly, it encapsulates the ways in which the surrogate is beholden to the contract and the arrangement. The responsibility of securing the pregnancy and seeing it through rests on the surrogate and her husband, who is a co-signatory—a signal that he controls rights to the surrogate's body. The mention of compensation is fleeting and hurried in the draft contract, as I have discussed in my research (Majumdar 2017). In Sama's (2012) research study on surrogacy in India, the contract becomes a 'disciplining tool', which is used by the clinics and the agents to scare the surrogate into conformity. In its research, Sama finds that varied elements of the contract alienate the surrogate from the arrangement and position her as a subsidiary. The language of the contract (which is mostly English and something the surrogate is not conversant in), the unavailability of legal counsel for the surrogate, and the vague references to her remuneration are elements of the contract that bind the surrogate to the arrangement in an inequitable way. In reality, as I discuss in my ethnography (Majumdar 2017), surrogacy lawyers engaged by the clinics often create an air of distrust with stories that feed into the fear of the surrogate reneging on the contract. This fear is primarily couched in terms of the surrogate's poverty and 'resulting greed' that make her untrustworthy, leading to a contract that is one-sided.

In the context of transnational commercial surrogacy, motherhood is the easiest target in the capitalist marketplace. Constructed within ideologies of altruism, motherhood in times of globalization is an underpaid, undervalued form of labour, meant for the creation and nurturance of the child that sustains patriarchal desires of biological continuity. So, motherhood as a social role is coming to occupy a global space of undervalued, exploited labour. This is, however, not a new process, but part of emerging forms of local–global experiments on the bodies of women from the Global South.

Altruistic Gift

Medical technology has successfully commoditized the body, evident from biomedical research in areas as diverse as DNA testing, organ transplants, and so on. The surrogacy arrangement is a result of this technological commodification. This is the reason for the moral unease that the surrogacy arrangement gives rise to. In order to hide and 'euphemise' its monetary aspect, laws in the UK and parts of the US insist on a surrogacy arrangement that does not involve the payment of money. The altruism attached to such an idea identifies the surrogacy arrangement as a 'gift exchange'. Laws in countries such as France and Germany completely ban surrogacy, while the UK accepts and endorses the altruistic form, just as Australia does in some of its states. The Warnock Report in the UK has outlawed surrogacy, except when it is done without any money changing hands. In the emerging climate of transnational surrogacy and the debate around the exploitation of poor women, more and more countries in Europe, including Spain, France, and Germany, began reviewing their legal stand on commercial and other forms of surrogacy and have imposed bans on it. However, there continue to be variations in laws and practices. In India, the new regulation introduced in 2016 also aims to allow only altruistic surrogacy arrangements. These and other aspects are discussed in detail in Chapter 5 of this book.

The insistence on altruism emerges from the intermingling of the intimate with commerce. As discussed in the previous section, the commodification of motherhood is an important part of the transnational commercial surrogacy arrangement. In 2010 during the hearing of cases regarding two German children born through surrogacy in India (see Chapter 5 of this book), the Supreme Court of India asked if children were a commodity being produced within the arrangement. The shock and anxiety that such 'associations' lead to have deep linkages with the idea of intimate relations that are for sale.

However, intimate relations and commercial transactions are part of each other. The positioning of these two spheres of human life as 'hostile worlds' does not necessarily mean that they do not meet. Commercial surrogacy is the perfect example of the ways in which the hostile worlds of intimacy and commerce meet and coexist. But this very obvious association means that within the surrogacy arrangement, the commercial transaction has to be 'euphemized' or hidden under a false pretext.

The 'gift' also straddles the hostile world of commerce and intimacy. In anthropological thought, the giving and receiving of a gift incurs obligation and reciprocity. The gift par excellence in south Asian Hindu practice is that of *kanyadaan* or the 'gift of the virgin', made during weddings along with other material gifts from the bride's father to the groom and his family. In Hindu philosophy such a gift is essential to attain salvation and is part of the householder's duties. The exchange of women and goods was the basis for kinship and familial ties in history, primarily because it facilitated the birth of kin and brought together tribes and communities in a relationship of marriage and blood. This is what forms the bulk of many traditional marriage rituals around the world even today.

However, within such rich symbolism and practice, commercial surrogacy is also designed as a 'gift of life' from the surrogate to the intended parents. Across cultural practices, the notion of the gift reappears in the practice of commercial surrogacy, adding to its complexity. According to Teman (2010), in Israel, where commercial surrogacy is encouraged and funded by the state as part of its pronatalist policy, the surrogate gifts 'motherhood' to the adoptive mother. In this sense she also transforms her into a mother. In the USA, many of the surrogates believe that they are giving the 'gift of life' to infertile couples who are unable to have children, a form of supreme sacrifice. In such imaginings, the language of payment and compensation barely enters the arrangement, even though it is one of the main reasons why women choose to enter commercial surrogacy as surrogates.

The couching of the contractual–commercial arrangement under the rubric of a gift exchange means that the surrogate is expected to hide her motivations under the guise of altruism. In the UK, where altruistic surrogacy arrangements are allowed by law, the compensation given to the surrogate has to be hidden under 'other' expenses for medication, food, and treatment. Altruism is intrinsically linked to the gift in case of commercial surrogacy. The gift is used for hiding the commercial transaction to be able to present the altruistic motivations and intentions of the commercial exchange. But, despite the overt use of the rhetoric of gift exchange, the surrogate's motivations are far more complex.

According to Levine (2003), American surrogates give the gift, and the altruism is primarily their responsibility. This form of altruism is also found in the study of Israeli surrogates by Teman (2010), who help 'birth a mother' rather than a child through the sacrificial act of carrying and giving birth to the surrogate baby. She must not tarnish the image of motherhood by explicitly stating that she does so for compensation. This is part of an elaborate design, wherein clinics encourage surrogates to think of their personal motivations in terms of altruism. In that sense, the personal and the socio-cultural come together in a neat package of gift-giving. However, there is sometimes conflict between the intended parents and the surrogates over treatment, miscarriage, or premature birth—or even when the intended parents (inevitably) sever ties with the surrogate after the birth of the child. This may be despite adherence to (and fulfilment of) the contract in its entirety. In her study of American surrogates, Berend (2010) finds that the obligation of the gift to return and cherish the tie that the surrogate has built is often broken by parents, leaving the surrogate in an emotional mess. Most often than not, the contract is invoked by the intended parents, while the surrogate grapples with her sense of 'surrogacy loss'. This is particularly acute as the surrogate has been trained to think of her motivations as altruistic and not commercial or 'fees paid for services rendered'.

In India, the gift and its complexities take a different turn. Socio-religious notions enter the 'training' of surrogates so as to make them believe that they occupy a place of virtue within the surrogacy arrangement. The stigma of the association between commercial surrogacy and sex work means that there is constant effort to de-stigmatize it and turn it into an act of piety and virtue. Hochschild (2011) finds the Indian surrogate mother grappling with two sets of identity:

'me' and 'not me'. The clinics and surrogacy agents encourage the construction of a dual self that grapples between the 'me', which takes pride in providing for her family and also providing 'help' to the intended parents, and the 'not me' that deals with the foetus she is carrying by treating it as part of her work that requires nurturance and sustenance.

Such a fractured identity marks the Indian surrogate's involvement in a transnational arrangement, where she deals with foreign couples with whom there are no shared ties of culture, class, or language. In that sense Hochschild (2011) notes that her alienation from herself and her work is complete. She is encouraged to see herself as a 'vessel' or 'room for rent', but does not give a gift, as much as receive one. According to Pande (2010), the Indian commercial surrogate is taught to believe in her 'good fortune' at being chosen to be part of a surrogacy arrangement that will bring her and her family material comfort. The surrogates in Pande's study were taught to worship and be thankful to 'surro-*dev*' (a term used by the surrogates in the study to designate a god-like stature to the surrogacy arrangement which they were part of), who brought them the good fortune of being chosen to participate in a commercial surrogacy arrangement.

The commercial transaction in transnational commercial surrogacy in India is overt and defines the participation of everyone concerned in the arrangement. The surrogate and her visible poverty cannot be hidden behind the façade of the gift of life. But her loyalty to the child and the intended parents is nonetheless unwavering. In case of foreign couples, the Indian surrogate is the impoverished woman from the Third World who requires sympathy and help. The gift is rechannelled as one that the intended parents give the surrogate as part of a 'philanthropic enterprise'. The surrogate is not as much altruistic as she is obligated and thankful for such charity and support; she becomes indebted to the intended couple in a relationship of dependence and complete subservience. The child she finally relinquishes to the intended parents is a 'thank-you' for all that they have done for her, including paying the compensation, the house they may have funded, or her children's education. At the same time, Pande (2011) notes, the act of philanthropy accompanies the construction of Indian surrogate mothers as 'greedy' for money. Clinics and surrogacy agents actively construct the surrogate as desiring money due to her poverty. Indian surrogates are trained to articulate altruistic motivations to quell their 'inherent greed' through worship and constructions of being good and honest women who are participating in surrogacy for their children. Hochschild (2011) finds Indian surrogates supplanting their connections to the foetus with the welfare of their own children for whose education and future they are undertaking surrogacy.

The ideology of the gift is inherently unequal and positions the surrogate and the intended parents not just in relationships of dependence, but also of exploitation. If the American surrogate feels the loss of her relationship with the intended parents after the birth of the child (whom she has nurtured just like the pregnancy), then the Indian surrogate is caught in a vortex of exploitation that obligates her to the arrangement. The Indian surrogate has no right to reject or demand affection and loyalty from her intended parents as they impose their right on her body and pregnancy, embedding her within a complicated discourse of altruism and gift giving. In many ways Indian surrogates become part of a traditional Indian system of the patron–client, where the indentured labour was beholden to his masters for their patronage and support, despite the hard work that he undertook. In that sense, Vora (2013) notes, the gift of life in Indian surrogacy is actually an exchange of 'life for life'. The surrogate and her family's survival are at stake in giving birth to the surrogate baby that she carries and nurtures.

It is to this idea of inequity and structured exploitation that we turn to next to understand the idea of surrogacy as labour.

Surrogacy as Labour

The identification of surrogacy as a form of paid work or labour has been part of academic debate for some time now. The fear of such an association means that commercial surrogacy, and motherhood, becomes aligned with work and money. This resurrects the idea of the 'hostile worlds' of money and intimacy. However, in trying to understand what it means to undertake commercial surrogacy we also need to look at the kinds of meaning and choices surrogates undertake in deciding to participate in the arrangement.

Pande's (2010) anthropological analysis into the lives of surrogate mothers living in the city of Anand in the western Indian state of Gujarat finds that the surrogates' narratives oscillate between justifying their roles of performing a 'special' kind of work to that of helping their families. She reiterates that in these narratives, while they wish to put forth a sense of their agency, they are unable to position their role as gestational surrogates as a form of labour. Pande believes that instead of identifying themselves as doing wage work, the women indulge in a form of misrepresentation wherein they find excuses to describe why they do what they do. This may include helping the family through a financially difficult period, securing their children's future, even invoking relations with the unborn child that places them in a position of nurturance and altruism vis-à-vis the completely commercial arrangement. What the surrogate mothers of Anand deny is their right to choose. They are clear about how they did not 'choose' to do what they did— circumstances compelled them into what Pande calls 'sexualised care work'.

This can be seen in the ways in which these women associate their work with stigma and a form of 'prostitution' of the body. Vora (2013) finds that the ART clinics actively socialize the gestational surrogate into believing that she is a mere receptacle, carrier, or, for lack of a better imagery, 'a room for rent'. She is made to believe that she has 'let out' her womb for a few months and has no claims to the occupant. Such rhetoric goes well with a commodity logic wherein the women are ready and willing surrogates after every successful pregnancy, thereby repeating a vicious cycle.

Majboori (desperation) was a recurring theme amongst the surrogate mothers trying to position their intention vis-à-vis surrogacy as dictated by financial need, altruistic motivations, or as a 'calling'. This was an accepted part of the rhetoric that came to dominate recruitment into surrogacy programmes. In this sense majboori as desperation and not necessity signals the channelling of life-changing, life-affirming routes. It does not necessarily draw from eulogized or normativized roles of being, as in the case of Pande's (2010) analysis, surrogates who placed their choice in the pursuit of higher goals.

The notion of choice does not enter into these narratives and ethnographic representations of surrogate women. In fact, they highlight what feminists have for long believed—that poor women's understanding of choice vis-à-vis their reproductive rights and, most importantly, their bodies is non-existent. In such an imagery of the surrogate, she comes across as a non-person actively involved in the misrecognition of her own self. The clinics, commissioning couples, and other institutions actively contribute to such a notion. Here the stigma of being 'carriers' and 'rooms for rent' is displaced only with a sense of purpose wherein the surrogates justify what they do by doing it for reasons which are altruistic in their narratives—doing it for the children's future, family, to offset husband's unemployment. This is a form of selflessness and entails huge sacrifice of their bodily and emotional integrity.

Thus, the poor Indian surrogate is 'needy' in media representations in the US—one who has to be pitied, and for whom money from the arrangement will go a long way to set up home and hearth. Markens (2007), in her insightful essay of media representations of poor American women who volunteer to be surrogates, finds that discursive media frames of the 'good' and the 'bad' surrogate means that the choices women make are placed in a hierarchy. In the USA, recent media debates on the global commerce in gestational surrogacy has brought into focus the exploitation of 'poor Third World wombs' by rich First World couples to have babies in exchange of inadequate compensation. The corresponding representations of American surrogates look at them as altruistic and undertaking to be pregnant for reasons other than monetary compensation. The emphasis is on how American surrogates are educated, well-off, and do not require to take up surrogacy to 'pay the bills'. On the other hand, there is a lot of negative publicity given to the poor, uneducated woman subsisting on welfare, who chooses to be a commercial surrogate.

It also resurrects debates about the commoditization of babies in a culture that celebrates pronatalism and the overt display of pregnancy as a 'haloed' state for most women. However, the same media narratives position the hiring of poor surrogates from the developed world as an act whereby they are 'empowered' to better their status in life. The 'bad' surrogate frame is thus replaced by the 'poor/needy' frame.

In fact, the poor American mother is similarly placed as the Indian surrogate with no luxury of making reproductive choices. For instance, the choice of a midwife for most poor American mothers is hardly a 'choice', unlike the upper-class women who can claim midwife services—in an increasingly medicalized environment—as part of exercising a consumer's choice. Motherhood as a form of neoliberal market agenda pervades the ways in which the 'right to choose' helps the sale of ARTs. By positioning some women within the sphere of consumerism they are given the illusion of choice between services and technologies. To be able to exercise your potential as a consumer demanding goods and services is the dream of modern living.

To seek legitimacy then becomes an important exercise. To 'choose' to enter surrogacy is marked by ideas of desperation. Surrogacy is *mehnat ka kaam* or hard labour, but involves a certain form of majboori that comes from both life circumstances and poverty.

Thus, choice itself comes to be constructed within interesting frames of agency—one that is purposely positioned by the surrogates themselves as 'choiceless'. The notion of choice represented in this narrative comes to occupy the landscape of Indian feminist activism and critique of how Indian surrogate mothers are coerced into entering TCGSA. This is why the focus on the surrogate mother's narratives has brought forth a more nuanced perspective regarding her choice and motivations, engaging specifically with the surrogate mother in different cultural contexts and the ways in which they understand their role in it.

In Rudrappa's (2015) insightful reading of Indian commercial surrogates working in Bangalore, she finds them providing an alternative and empowering narrative for entering the arrangement. Threatened with constant sexual harassment and low pay in inhumane conditions, many of the surrogates had left work in garment factories to choose surrogacy. They found the work to be more respectable and with better pay—not to mention the friendlier working conditions. Rudrappa finds that the commercial surrogates move away from tough sweat shop conditions and constant precariousness of their safety on the factory floor to surrogacy, which promises to be a better option.

This is similar to findings in my study (Majumdar 2018) of the ways in which many of the paid domestic workers in Delhi chose surrogacy to escape the precariousness of low pay and the undignified labour of working at people's homes. Even though surrogacy is stigmatising, ironically, so is paid domestic work. Cleaning other people's homes comes with notions of pollution that women who work as maids incur on a daily basis. Given the option, many of the domestic servants preferred surrogacy. The terms of engagement expected them to stay at home during the pregnancy (unlike in Bangalore, Mumbai, and Anand), with their families. The compensation was better and the stigma of being a commercial surrogate could be managed better than that of being a maid. In Sama's (2012) study commercial surrogates would lie about their surrogate pregnancy to extended family; they would either shift to another city for the period or claim to have had a miscarriage after the delivery.

★★★

The notion of surrogacy as labour has far-reaching consequences for policy, provided that clinics, intended parents, and surrogates themselves believe that they do so. Identifying their role as surrogates within the prism of work will bring equitable pay and labour benefits for commercial surrogates. But as long as it is couched in terms of altruism, gift-giving, and motherhood, the commercial surrogate in India will perhaps continue to be part of a hierarchical arrangement.

4

The Parents
Kinship in the Making

The TCGSA brings together intended parents, surrogate mothers, egg and sperm donors, and IVF specialists in a carefully crafted story of parenthood. The child born of the arrangement is an amalgamation of elements, influences, and the genetic contribution of more than the traditional heterosexual dyadic union of man and woman. With the help of ARTs, preferably the IVF technique, an artificially fertilized embryo is implanted into the womb of a woman who carries the foetus to term. The possibilities of 'making parents' seem to be endless in new-age procreation.

In TCGSA, parents and parenthood are made and unmade. The idea of parenthood is under scrutiny due to the artificial mode of reproduction through IVF, the participation of the anonymous egg/sperm donor, and the presence of a surrogate. Between the conflict of two–three potential mothers and the construction of gene-biology, the commercial gestational surrogacy arrangement presents unique dilemmas. The study of the relationship between genes and biology has received the most attention, and in the context of transnational surrogacy the interface of race and procreation, as well as the engagement of gay families have been researched about extensively.

At the foundation of the commercial gestational surrogacy arrangement are infertile couples, seeking technological interventions to have a child. The desire for biological progeny is definitely part of why the arrangement takes place. Infertility also remains the primary reason why surrogates may choose to enter the arrangement. Surrogates rationalize their participation by articulating that they are helping the infertile couples have a child. This helps them position their motivations in an altruistic mode. However, it is importantly to note that the manufacturing of ideas regarding genes and biology are far more complicated.

Considering that ideas regarding biology, blood, and genes have been and are being questioned within cultural–social understandings of the same, when referring to genes here I mean a substance that may be tracked through a DNA test.

Blood, Biology, and Genes

In commercial gestational surrogacy, the idea of biology is predominant through the positioning of genes in opposition to nurturance. Remember, the idea of biology is not so clear-cut as the surrogate fulfils an important role, which is closely linked to the natural–biological ties between mother and child.

In their positioning of surrogacy and genes to the intended parents and to the surrogate, the IVF specialist employs different kinds of rhetoric. Reportedly, the genetic tie to the child through sperm and/or egg is highlighted to the intended parents—stressing on their genetic contribution—while surrogates are constantly told that they share no genetic links to the child by exaggerating the connections the egg and sperm share with the intended parents (Menon 2012).

Genes are an important part of the conversation on parenthood in commercial surrogacy. They embody the social understanding of biology in constructive ways. The gene is imagined in commercial surrogacy in conflicted ways through a complicated process of making kin. Here, the identification and desire to create parents involves sustained work by IVF specialists, surrogates, agents, and intended parents.

The ARTs and IVF clinics systematically 'choreograph' parenthood, especially in cases where third-party participants such as egg and sperm donors are involved. Both Thompson (2005) and Bharadwaj (2003) study the different kinds of choreographies involved in IVF clinics in the USA and India respectively that facilitate kinship and parenthood. Parents-to-be must manage their linkages to the child, especially when the donors may themselves be kin. This is especially acute in case of egg and sperm donors, as the idea of genes is constructed in relation to genetic matter in sperm and egg. According to Bharadwaj (2003), IVF specialists in India help couples maintain secrecy about the use of anonymous donor sperm due to the stigma attached to the idea of third-party reproduction. IVF specialists direct intended parents' attention towards suitable/unsuitable donors, based on kinship relations. In case of gestational surrogacy, the identification of motherhood gets complicated between the egg donor, surrogate, and the adoptive-intended mother.

Thus, as discussed in Majumdar (2017), in case of altruistic surrogacy arrangements—wherein couples often opt for surrogates and donors from amongst close or distant kin—IVF specialists suggest kin who could qualify as potential surrogates. This form of sifting is not only based on medical factors but is also influenced by local cultural kinship values. So, for instance, in North India, IVF specialists would recommend women from the intended mother's family as suitable for surrogacy, rather than women from the intended father's family. Ideas of incest and marriage influence eligibility. The intended father's sister is not a likely candidate for surrogacy due to the supposed linkages with incest, even though it is an asexual arrangement. On the other hand, the intended mother's mother or sister are prefect candidates for surrogacy as they come from a family which is in an inferior position to the intended father's family—the position of wife-givers. As per North Indian kinship ideologies, wife-takers or the groom's side is superior to the wife-givers or the bride's side. Thus, the reproductive potential of a woman from the wife-giver's side is suitable for the surrogacy arrangement because the hierarchy is maintained. Interestingly, one of the first surrogacy arrangements in India involved a woman who became a gestate for her infertile daughter.

Such local–cultural positioning of genes and blood relationships amongst medical doctors is referred to as 'gene sutra' by Bharadwaj (2003), wherein IVF specialists participate in making kin through third-party reproduction. However, I also suggest that IVF specialists fall upon local notions of kinship and marriage to act as 'matchmakers' involved in creating viable matches of donors and surrogates with intended parents. Just like marriage matchmakers seek suitable familial links to facilitate a suitable match and the birth of suitable progeny, IVF specialists perform genetic matching based on ideas of the familial to perform acts of kinship and kinning. Biology and blood are accordingly imagined in the construction of the familial. However, in TCGSA, race and cross-cultural kinship ideologies collide in interesting ways to give meaning to parenthood.

Race and Surrogacy

The interplay of race and kinship plays most pre-dominantly in transnational commercial surrogacy. It is important to note here that the racial intermingling—through the Indian surrogate and the large number of foreign couples—has led to a deeper and more significant conversation regarding cultural understanding of kinship and reproduction.

In Deomampo's (2016) work, she finds white American and European intended parents engage in 'othering' the Indian commercial surrogate. This is done primarily through the frames of treating her as a distant impoverished woman, whom they are helping overcome financial distress. This 'othering' helps the intended parents distance their child from the surrogate's role of gestate and position themselves as 'philanthropic'.

Many of the foreign gay couples having children through surrogacy in India have been grappling with the race of the surrogate. For many of them the genetic tie to the egg donor is more important, who is anonymous in most cases. They privilege the ties their children share with the anonymous egg donor to the ties with the instantly recognizable surrogate. Alternatively, the gay father recognizes India as a 'culture and country', as the mother of his children, rather than explicitly identifying the Indian gestational surrogate as the mother. Yet, she could not be completely dismissed as many of the couples wanted to keep track of other couples who had children from the same surrogate or egg donor to avoid the probability of the children becoming intimate later in their lives for fear of incest.

Racial differences also play out in other forms of distinction such as ethnicity and caste. For instance, in Teman's (2010) study of Israeli surrogates and adoptive mothers, Israeli Jew intended couples preferred Jews as egg donors, but Israeli Arab women could only be eligible as surrogates. This was primarily because the idea of gestation within gestational surrogacy is constructed as having a minor role to play in determining the genetic make-up of the child. Similarly, Pande (2014) finds Indian couples, especially NRIs, seeking surrogates from their own caste group or religion. Such filtering was especially important as the choice of the gestate by Indian couples was influenced by the diet and religion of the surrogate, which the foetus would be subjected to during the nine months of the pregnancy.

Compared to the Israeli surrogates in Teman's study who took credit for making mothers by giving birth to children for infertile women, the Indian surrogates in Pande's study took credit for 'nurturing' the child in their womb through the labour of pregnancy and gestation.

Visible Gay Family

Official statistics on the number of people who have come to India to have children through transnational commercial surrogacy are unavailable, and at best informal (generated by individual clinics). The nature of the industry and the ambiguity of purpose (neither strictly medical, nor tourist visa-qualified before 2013) has led to a lack of statistics, especially of the number of gay couples coming to India to have babies. Though there are no official estimates on the number of gay couples coming to India for surrogacy, the number is large enough to warrant attention. The ICMR is quick to point out that it has never given fillip to this trend. In its Draft Guidelines surrogacy is restricted only to '"couple" [meaning] two persons living together and having a sexual relationship that is legal in India'. Yet, the frequency with which foreign gay couples are spoken of in reportage on surrogacy in India points towards another side of the surrogacy story—one in which gay couples are openly proclaiming their right to exercise their reproductive choice.

Unwilling to be marginalized as 'dysfertile', gay couples are in many ways redefining the mainstream by using the alternative of surrogacy to have children. Prohibited from legally adopting children in not only their own countries, but transnationally as well, couples from Australia, the USA, and some European countries are coming to India to fulfil a lifelong dream. However, in recent times, gay couples have been allowed to get married and adopt in some of these countries.

Mass media—electronic and print—regularly profile gay couples with newborns and their IVF doctors in different cities of India. Their representations of transnational commercial surrogacy in India also portray the gay couple in the a number frames: the happy couple solemnizing their long-time relationship (there is an insistence on mentioning the duration of the relationship, which in many ways panders to stereotypes of the promiscuous gay); the consumer of the reproductive tourism industry in India; and the hapless victim of nations unable to understand the growing reach of ARTs. Stories of gay single fathers and gay couples stuck in no-man's land with their newborns suggest that their nations—mostly European countries where surrogacy is not legal—are not very welcome to the idea of gay parents. Yet, it is interesting to see how mass media narratives position the gay family—in long-term relationships with one partner and with children through ARTs and not from adoption, giving it the biological tinge. Each child born through surrogacy is linked to one of the fathers, and the genetic mother is either a close friend or an anonymous donor. The mother is also invariably more than one—the surrogate and the egg donor—at least in the case of transnational commercial surrogacy in India.

Yet, the media attention on the 'particularities' that highlight the ability of gay men to parent (as well as the heterosexuals) attempts to point towards their 'strangeness'. The costs of visibility, openness, and the ability to exercise choice are also undermined in the ways in which gay couples have to undergo, as quoted in an Indian daily, 'nursery training to learn parenting'. The desire to be 'normal' and like everyone else, as highlighted by the media, is not necessarily positive; the fact that couples/individuals get stuck in India with their babies due to the refusal of their nations to extend citizenship to the child is not evident in subtexts of 'sexuality' either.

Several nations are also witnessing a moral churning of sorts as far as the gestation of their future generations is concerned. Germany, Norway, Spain, Japan, France, Hungary, and Saudi Arabia either do not recognize surrogacy or are not amenable to the idea of gay couples raising babies. Yet, the visibility of gay parents as opposed to heterosexual couples having surrogate babies seems to suggest a healthy number of gay couples coming into the country. This visibility was channelized by many of these couples in their favour—in countries including Australia, the US, and the UK—to fight for marriage equality. This visibility is part of the more aggressive fight for identification, and the family born through transnational commercial surrogacy helps gay couples and singles overcome the stigma of their social status as a 'non-community', a term used by Pervez Mody (2008) to describe young couples in India who elope and are excluded from their respective communities in the process. To be a 'non-community' is to reclaim a social public space that was earlier denied to the eloping couple or gay couple by the same legitimating state and social practices.

It was thus that the 2013 directive—forbidding couples who were not heterosexual and married from coming to India to contract a surrogacy arrangement—added to the institutionalized sanctions that the Indian state had brought in in relation to homosexuality in

India. A draconian clause in the Indian Penal Code (IPC), Section 377, made homosexuality, along with bestiality and sodomy, a criminal offence. A few years back the section on homosexuality as a part of 'unnatural' sex within the IPC was struck down by the Indian courts. But the law was reinstated in 2014 by the Indian Supreme Court which was widely read as a regressive move. Thus, even though foreign gay couples were able to contract a surrogacy arrangement in India till the 2013 directive came into effect, Indian gay couples were unable to access the same surrogacy services. Fighting social prejudice and familial dis-approval which often takes a violent form, the terrain of gay activism in India has a long way to go. However, with the recent judgment of the Supreme Court decriminalizing 'unnatural' sexual acts—and, in effect, legalizing homosexuality—the road towards claiming rights and social acceptance has become more accessible. Anurag Kashyap, Mumbai-based gay rights activist speaks of how legitimacy is priority number one for the gay community in India; children and access to surrogacy remain a cherished goal.

IVF clinics, too, clearly discriminate not only between heterosexual and gay, but also between the Indian gay couple and the Western gay couple. Some clinics such as the infamous Akanksha clinic in Anand, Gujarat, openly reject gay couples as candidates for surrogacy. Other clinics woo Western gay couples due to their financial clout.

The stigma attached to the heterosexual couples accessing ARTs and transnational commercial surrogacy also forces gay couples to be invisible, again, strangely, due to the same legitimating social practices that value sexual reproduction within marriage as haloed. This is despite the state's overt attempts to legitimate the child born to the heterosexual couple through ARTs. Thus, the 'hush-hush' nature of gay couples accessing surrogacy transnationally means that when they seek official legitimacy for their children— for processing citizenship papers in India—the couples have to position themselves as single men. Just as marriage is a necessity for the heterosexual couple to seek children through surrogacy, hiding their sexuality and relationship status is necessary for the homosexual couples to have children in India through surrogacy.

Imagining the Gay Family

An interesting element of the gay family, formed through transnational commercial surrogacy, is the way in which genes and genetic ties are understood. The number of gay men coming to India to have children through surrogacy has been higher than the number of lesbian women because the latter have the ability to gestate a pregnancy. Many of the gay couples make sense of their linkages with their newborn through the concept of the 'non-bio dad'. Even though both partners provide their sperm to the surrogate pregnancy, the person whose sperm leads to fertilization is the one identified in the official birth certificate. This means that despite not wanting to, the partner who is not genetically connected to the child has to identify himself in order to co-parent and legally adopt the newborn. This includes copious amounts of paperwork for many couples back home to give legitimacy to their relationship as a couple for parenting and parenthood. The 'non-bio dad' then becomes a problematic space of engagement for the gay couples trying to avoid questions regarding genetic ties to the child. Interestingly, many of the gay couples would come back for a second pregnancy to ensure that both partners had genetic links to at least one of their children, and neither of them was in the difficult position, legally, of being a non-bio dad, in case one of them dies intestate without granting parental rights to his partner (Majumdar 2017). In cases mentioned during my fieldwork, a gay man in Australia had lost parental rights to his child after his partner died, as the latter was the genetic father and did not leave a will granting parental rights to his partner. Having genetic ties to their child (even if they are excluded from having any with the other child) gives some sense of security to the couple. This is the reason why the desire for marriage equality has become louder—for the sake of the children and families these couples are bringing up. At the time of writing this book, Australia had just voted in favour of marriage equality in a mammoth nation–wide referendum.

ARTs are providing us with the option of choosing our families, beyond those we are destined to be part of by the accident of birth. They are in no way a negation to biology or sexual procreation, nor a reaffirmation of the same. The notion of 'choice' is an important part of gay relationships and parenting. However, the way the state constructs relationships (often in knots, as is evident) emerging from ARTs tends to place them in the rhetoric of biology. Choosing ARTs to have children in many ways signifies both the appropriation of the dominant ideology of heterosexual procreation as well as pandering to a norm that places biology at the core of kinship.

Kath Weston (1991) has referred to how the gay family is positioned against the straight family in opposition to the notions of blood and biology. Here, the procreative relationship is at the core of kinship and all others are based on the non–procreative intent. The 'real' family is the one stemming from biology and the 'non-family' is the one forged through choice. This hierarchy embeds itself within state and popular discourse—making gay and single parent families as 'alternatives' to the norm.

Butler (2002) finds that the gay marriage question brings state control into the world of sexual relations and tries to position them in straitjacket terms of heterosexuality. She also contests that fighting for equal rights in marriage in some ways comes to represent the urge to fall in with the 'norm'—that being married is the only way to be. Extending one norm to those who were 'ab-normal' is not usurping it, but falling prey to its universalizing, totalizing influence. And this is exactly what has been happening with reproductive technologies. Their legitimation, however, has come unstuck in its adherence and loyalty to the norm, while at the same time hiding its revolutionary potential.

Gay couples having families through ARTs are families of choice; they are not at any point trying to create or be part of the mainstream, rather they are redefining the mainstream. By wanting children— whether through adoption or through ARTs, or by juxtaposing the two in a completely new way—gay couples are saying that they have every right to parent, just as straight couples do. And while the right to marry is still underway in some countries—and completely elusive in some others—that has not stopped the family of choice to assert that it 'chose' and did not follow a normativizing agenda.

However, the desire for biological progeny amongst gay couples has become a part of the course of their life by normativizing it. According to Riggs and Due (2017), this form of normalizing of the desire for genetic connectedness with their children is like pandering to a heteronormative agenda—just like Butler's (2002) conceptualization of gay marriage. As 'repropreneurs' (conceptualized by Krolokke and Pant [2012]), gay couples 'ignore' or are unwilling to engage with the problematic spaces of exploitation and choice that surrogates operate within. According to Riggs and Due (2017), this is deeply problematic and complicates the idea of the gay family and kinship further.

Riggs and Due (2017) suggest that parenting and kinship should be engaged with in all its complexity. This means that in identifying that choice, markets, human rights, and commodification collide in unsavoury and revolutionary ways in transnational commercial surrogacy.

★★★

This chapter looked at the ways in which parenthood and kinship are essential elements to the transnational commercial surrogacy arrangement. The focus was on the arrangement especially from the standpoint of the ways in which motherhood and fatherhood were constructed within a narrative of biology and blood, which were further contradicted and complicated by notions of race, choice, and gender. It is to these dilemmas that this chapter was addressed.

5

The Law

Making Legislative Sense of Commercial Surrogacy

Since 2010, when the ICMR made its draft regulation of the ARTs bill public, there has been regular commentary and criticism of the bill through its many avatars. This chapter looks at the bill, focusing on specific elements of the legal discourse on commercial surrogacy in India. The aim is to inform and discuss ethical and moral questions that transnational commercial surrogacy has raised in India.

As of August 2017, the Parliamentary Committee had extensive discussions on the suggested Surrogacy Bill of 2016, recommending important amendments. The current bill is a 'breakaway' from the ARTs Bill of 2015, signalling the state's desire to ban commercial surrogacy altogether. The bill is not an Act, yet, and every new deliberation adds to the complexities of the bill.

The 102nd Report of the Parliamentary Standing Committee (PSC 2017) was released in August 2017, and it involved discussions of all stakeholders and the Surrogacy Bill of 2016. Civil society participants, government ministries, IVF specialists, gynaecology and obstetrics societies, surrogacy lawyers, commissioning couples, and surrogates were part of the deliberations. Briefly, the PSC recommends a reengagement with surrogacy in terms of altruism–commercialization, compensation, and access.

The Report makes an important intervention by questioning the meaning of an 'altruistic' surrogacy arrangement by stating two important issues. One, altruism involves payment for the IVF procedure, medicine, and nutrition; however, denying the surrogate compensation for her reproductive labour is unfair. The committee was in favour of developing a compensatory surrogacy system that aimed to provide healthcare and compensation to surrogates. Second, the dependence on kin to volunteer for an altruistic surrogacy arrangement was fraught with issues of familial coercion and stigma associated with infertility. The committee was unsure of whether the infertile couple would be willing to share their infertility with their family and also if, in a situation of increasing small, nuclear families, kin would be willing to undertake a pregnancy to later relinquish the child.

The suggestion to look at a compensatory mode for surrogacy in India meant, more importantly, that the surrogate will be treated equitably; she would be provided with insurance, and her post delivery health would be monitored for up to three months. In many ways such suggestions aimed to move away from a commercialized, industry model of surrogacy in India, recommending a more equitable arrangement for all concerned, especially the child and the surrogate.

The PSC noted that access to surrogacy in India, though open to Indian citizens, cannot be discriminatory to unmarried couples (as live-in couples are also identified as legitimate), single individuals, and foreigners. This also meant that the parameters for opting for surrogacy were to be made more stringent, with five years of medically proven infertility after marriage and the advice to promote adoption before surrogacy as a viable option. This implied that the PSC was also inclined to be critical of surrogacy as an option to earn a living out of poverty, in turn suggesting to the National Commission for Women to encourage vocational training and job creation amongst women belonging to a lower socio-economic category who act as surrogates.

The current deliberations have come through after decade-long deliberations and activism on transnational commercial surrogacy in India. Some of these issues and deliberations have been discussed later in the chapter.

Ban or No Ban

The important part of the debate regarding commercial surrogacy is centred on the issue of executing a ban, or not. Internationally, many countries have opted for partial bans (prohibiting only the commercial form), while others have executed a complete ban (neither commercial nor altruistic surrogacy). In India, the ARTs regulation bill always recommended regulating commercial surrogacy, the language of a ban never existed. The surrogacy bill of 2016 brought the idea of a ban to the centre stage.

The conversation surrounding the ban on surrogacy is primarily consumed with its linkages to commerce. The act of 'hiring' and 'renting out' one's body has always led to questions regarding ethics and morality. The ARTs Bill of 2010 deals with the issue of payment as 'compensation' to the surrogate for the services rendered. Thus, it mentions that the couple hiring the surrogate should bear the expenses incurred in the arrangement including medicine, hospital visits, and insurance. The contours of the compensation identify costs linked to the 'treatment' or the use of the technology and the kind of medical intervention that the doctor provides, but none regarding the labour that the surrogate undertakes. In many ways the surrogate is subsumed within the technology and seen as an appendage to the miraculous 'cure' rendered by the ARTs. Such a representation has a dual purpose: first, the delineation of surrogacy from its discomfiting commercial linkages; and second, the focus on technological prowess, giving the medical practitioner more power and control over the arrangement and its monetary modalities.

The ways in which a 'ban' is envisioned, therefore, necessarily involves the invocation of bodily integrity. In countries such as Germany, France, and Sweden, amongst others where surrogacy is banned in entirety, the idea of the body has different legal–cultural meanings. In France, the human body is indissoluble, making it impossible for it to be broken down and bartered, thereby making both organ donation and surrogacy impermissible by law. In Sweden, the maternal body is 'whole', especially in its gestational role. The woman who carries the child for nine months in her womb is always the mother. Egg donation may be possible but in case of surrogacy, the surrogate is the mother and therefore the commercial exchange of a child is a morally problematic concept. In Germany, Spain, and UK (where altruistic surrogacy is allowed), similar concerns regarding the maternal body determine questions of banning the practice.

In India, the Surrogacy Bill 2016 is particular in this regard. Though not made available publicly, the primary contours of the bill sought to separate it from the ARTs Bill in an important signal to the state's changed stance towards surrogacy. It's important to understand that the ways in which surrogacy comes to be understood in the new bill necessitates its ban. Thus, the discourse surrounding the new bill positions commercial surrogacy as an exploitative practice that renders Indian women as subjects of economic exploitation, especially by foreigners. The bill identifies the commercial hiring of surrogates as a morally reprehensible act, similar to the view prevalent in Germany and Scandinavia that positions motherhood as absolute. However, there is an important difference here—the identification of the 'womb for rent' becomes the problematic trope for commercial surrogacy. Not only is motherhood threatened, the repository of the family's line and descent is also invaded upon in the representation of the womb as commercially exchangeable.

This is seen particularly in the way in which altruistic surrogacy is endorsed as the only viable form of engaging a surrogate. Altruistic surrogacy, in the way in which it is practiced in India, involves kin seeking support from the female members to help fulfil the role of a surrogate. Thus, altruism promises not only the euphemization of commerce, compensation, and renting, but also retains the womb that births kin within the familial. The Surrogacy Bill of 2016 in many ways is a legislation regarding the acceptable contours of the Indian family.

Rao (2012) is one of the few open critics of commercial surrogacy in India, linking it with ideas of reproductive slavery, wherein poor women are exploited to carry children for richer, upper-caste couples from India and other parts of the world. He has advocated a ban on commercial surrogacy, adding that only altruistic arrangements should be allowed.

Critiquing the Law

The criticism of legislation under construction in the area of ARTs has been varied and the subject of much public debate. Since its very first avatar in 2008, the Regulation of Assisted Reproductive Technologies Bill has been subject to intense scrutiny. As mentioned in the beginning of this chapter, the 2010 version of the bill received the most feedback and critique, primarily because it was made available to the public.

Essentially, the critique against the bill focused on three primary ideas: one, the access to ARTs; two, the representation of parenthood and biology; and three, the positioning of the surrogate within the bill. Through the bill, ARTs such as IVF and ICSI were positioned as larger and more important than the human participants accessing it. While identifying it as a saviour technology, the bill becomes a champion of the technology—in many ways selling it to particular constituencies—rather than championing its universal use. Earlier drafts of the bill, especially back in 2008, had revolutionary potential in their conceptualization of access to ARTs. These drafts sought to extend the use of the technology to single parents and unmarried couples, which left sexuality ambiguous. And even though the bill is 'liberal' in its consideration of the unmarried couple within the norms of eligibility to have a child through the use of ARTs, it manages to overturn this when identifying the rights of the child born of ARTs. '"Unmarried couple" means two persons, both of marriageable age, living together with mutual consent but without getting married, in a relationship that is legal in the country/ countries of which they are citizens' (ICMR 2010). Some of these were later watered down to specify that only married couples could access the technology. The point of access is an important counter to the ARTs Bill especially amongst feminists and civil society activists.

The form of social valuation that marks the question of access is later seen in the Ministry of External Affairs memo regarding the granting of medical visas to foreigners coming to India to contract surrogacy arrangements. The memo issued in 2013 made the surrogacy arrangement accessible only to heterosexual married couples, who had been married for at least two years. This effectively ruled out single parents-to-be and gay couples from contracting a surrogacy arrangement with Indian surrogates and clinics.

The question of access is also linked to the idea of parenthood and the state–legal endorsement of particular forms of parenthood. In the Law Commission's report on surrogacy, the idea of infertility as a social burden on married couples points towards the tacit acknowledgement of a culture that positions biological parenthood as an important social signifier of completeness and fulfilment.

The bill drew much criticism for its definition of parents/couples. It's definition of the biological parent as genetic parents makes parentage a biologically determined tie which is, however, not replicated in the very 'social' definition of the 'couple' as 'two persons living together and having a sexual relationship that is legal in India'. The biological essentialism inherent in these definitions meant that ARTs were seen as the only way to have a family in case of infertility—thereby negating the option of adopting a child. The bill also tries to create legitimacy for the technology by placing the child born through it at par with the child born of sexual relations within a marriage—the 'normal' way. 'A child born to a married couple through the use of assisted reproductive technology shall be presumed to be the legitimate child of the couple, having been born in wedlock and with the consent of both spouses, and shall have identical rights as a legitimate child born through sexual intercourse' (ICMR 2010).

At the same time, access to ARTs was defined by various other forms of concerns. By replicating a 'natural' tie, the bill tries to represent the technology as the best way to have children. In the repeated references to 'a child of one's own', adoption as a suitable, alternative mode of having children is not suggested. This is seen the most in the way the idea of 'genes' is privileged. In a medico-technological dominated world, the definition of 'one's own' has come to be understood within scientific paradigms of genes and DNA. The ICMR Bill, too, privileges the same rule. The break-up of the pregnancy achieved through ARTs into more than two components (in which one/both of them will remain anonymous) is another form of privileging. It maintains that the anonymous gamete donors'/providers' identities should be kept anonymous and stored in separate records, to be maintained by the ART Banks. In case of known donors such as the husband and wife, the Bill makes a distinction between the husband's sperm and that of the anonymous provider's.

This is seen in the way infertility comes to be increasingly recognized in medico-technological terms, away from its social moorings. The medicalization of pregnancy displaces the human actors and makes them part of the technology.

The surrogate is treated as part of the technology and treatment, thereby denying her her basic rights. The primary critique here is on the lack of many provisions vis-à-vis the surrogate, including the missing discussion of the surrogacy contract, the absence of safeguards in relation to the surrogate's health, the silence on the surrogate's compensation, and the lack of recognition given to the surrogate in the birth of the child. Due to the profile of the Indian surrogate— mostly poor women willing to gestate due to the 'large' monetary incentives—they escape the notice of the bill as individuals jeopardizing their physical and mental health to enter into the transaction.

The issue of the health of the surrogate is never duly addressed. The number of IVF cycles a surrogate can undergo to get pregnant and to the number of pregnancies she actually goes through are never really fleshed out. The insistence on having a separate egg donor and surrogate, even in cases where the adoptive/ social mother is unable to generate her own eggs and in the case of gay couples, is most problematic in most of the feminist critiques. This is an attempt to usurp the surrogate from having any right on the child and also from being able to exercise the choice to terminate the pregnancy. Instead, as a gestational mother, she has to be willing to subject her body to the manipulations of ARTs that may be potentially harmful.

This is further complicated by the mention of compensation to the surrogate; yet, no clear benchmarks are given for the kind of compensation to be given. Thus, the contract is left open-ended for the benefit of the couples (many of whom are foreigners) and middlemen to exploit to their advantage. The bill only mentions:

All expenses including those related to insurance if available, of the surrogate related to a pregnancy achieved in furtherance of assisted reproductive technology shall, during the period of the pregnancy and after delivery as per the medical advice, and till the child is ready to be delivered as per medical advice, to the biological parent or parents, shall be borne by the couple or individual seeking surrogacy.

Feminist Critique of the Legislation on ARTs and Surrogacy

Sama (2009) finds the exclusivity of the ARTs Bill discriminatory for homosexual couples or single parents who may want to use the technology to have a child. The Sama critique finds the above clause under 'Determination of status of the child' more of a violation than a recognition. As per their critique, this clause seems to identify only the child born of the marital tie as 'eligible' for rights, privileging one tie and simultaneously excluding single parents and homosexual couples from having children through ARTs.

The Sama (2009) critique finds the social connotations to a medical treatment very disturbing. Thus, in the draft Bill, '"artificial insemination" means the procedure of artificially transferring semen into the reproductive system of a woman and includes insemination with the husband's semen or with donor sperm', thereby qualifying the husband's sperm as different from the donor sperm, but not necessarily doing the same in case of oocytes. This privileges patrilineal descent, granting legitimacy to the father and the importance of descent genetically through him. And because gestational surrogacy has already disaggregated motherhood, eggs and gestation are not identified as important markers for parenthood, legally.

However, within a bill that is selling the technology because it will help a couple have 'one's own' child, such value judgments are to be expected.

The promotion of gestational surrogacy over the simpler IUI, where the surrogate also donates her eggs, is part of a medical logic that wishes to promote the interests of the clinic and of 'more' technology. This is critiqued by many of the feminists as subordinating the surrogate's health interests for the demands of the technology.

The draft Bill is fertile ground for the entry of intermediaries such as surrogacy agents, medical tourism agencies, and middlemen to exploit the right to adequate compensation and further exploitation. Sama (2009) finds the following areas of major oversight on the part of the drafting committee:

1. eligibility and age for becoming a surrogate;
2. contract between the surrogate and the couple;
3. exploitative role played by 'middle-men' and intermediaries in surrogacy arrangements;
4. special safeguards and special terms of agreement for surrogates commissioned by foreigners;
5. role of the semen bank in the payments made to the surrogate;
6. other health risks that surrogates are vulnerable to;
7. health insurance and legal aid for the surrogate;

8. other rights of the surrogate and guardianship; and
9. screening of the intended couples.

The Peculiar Cases of the Balaz Twins and Baby Manji

In 2008 and 2009 two subsequent cases were in the news for a considerable period of time. Both the cases had certain common elements: they involved infants born of Indian surrogate mothers who had been hired by their foreign parents; the children born in both cases were stuck in no-man's land due to legal complications; and the cases brought into focus the legal and ethical loopholes that commercial surrogacy posed for the one person the arrangement was meant for—the child.

For Baby Manji—the Japanese girl born of the eggs of an unknown Indian donor and the sperm of her father, Ikufumi Yamada—the legal hassles began with the Japanese government refusing to process her citizenship and an Indian NGO filing a suit on ethical grounds. Parallels with the American Baby M case (discussed in the 'Introduction' of this book), both in the press and in legal reports, are more relevant in the sense that both the cases garnered a lot of media attention rather than in their basic outlines. Manji's status as a prospective Japanese citizen was hampered due to the ambiguous status surrogacy has in Japan—banned by the Society of Obstetricians and Gynaecologists—but with no legal provision dealing with it. Besides, with the Yamadas getting divorced before Manji's birth, the wife, Yuki, had relinquished her rights over the unborn child as she had no genetic links to her, leaving Ikufumi, the genetic father, in a bind as India does not allow single men to adopt girl children. A public interest litigation filed by an Indian child rights NGO questioned his motives vis-à-vis the child. Ikufumi's mother had to step in as the proxy mother to be able to take the child back to Japan. Ultimately, Japan relented after diplomatic missions with India and gave Manji the passport she needed to be home.

Stance of Countries vis-à-vis Surrogacy—Commercial and Altruistic[#]

Countries that prohibit surrogacy	France, Germany, Italy, Norway, Singapore, Spain, Sweden, Vietnam, Iceland
Countries where commercial surrogacy is prohibited (but altruistic surrogacy is legal)	Canada, China, Israel, UK, Hong Kong, Hungary
Countries where surrogacy in every form is legal	India*, Russia, Ukraine, Georgia, Thailand*, South Africa

(Cont'd)

Selective prohibition/ ambiguous status	Australia (Queensland—prohibits surrogacy; Victoria, Tasmania, Australian Capital Territory, and South Australia—prohibit commercial surrogacy); USA (California, Arkansas, Florida, Illinois, Nevada, New Hampshire, Texas, Utah and Virginia—allow, but regulate surrogacy); Japan (looking to ban/legalize surrogacy—banned by the Society of Gynaecologists and Obstetricians); UAE (the Sharia does not encourage surrogacy, but is not averse to women using ARTs)

Notes: #Altruistic surrogacy involves the practice of surrogacy without taking compensation for the gestation. Often undertaken between close kin, the commissioning couple often pay for the treatment, but not for 'hiring the womb' (discussed in Chapter 3).
★Thailand banned commercial surrogacy for foreigners in 2015, and India has a bill banning commercial surrogacy, which is awaiting parliamentary approval.
Source: Sama Resource Group for Women and Health (2010), *Regulation of Surrogacy in Indian Context*. New Delhi: Sama.

The Balaz Twins, discussed in the national media from early 2009 to early 2010, were not so lucky. They had to undergo long, protracted legal negotiations till the trial ended with a positive judgment for the twins.

In 2008 German nationals Jan Balaz and Suzanne Lohle came to India to become parents. For Balaz and Lohle, surrogacy was the only route available after every other ART had failed to deliver. The gestational surrogate, Martha Christy, carried the foetus from Balaz's sperm and the egg of an anonymous Indian donor to full term, after which—as per the requirements of the contract—she handed the babies over to Balaz in exchange for compensation. The entire transaction was negotiated and carried out at an infertility clinic in Gujarat. However, Balaz was unable to take the children to Germany, his country of residence, because it prohibits surrogacy in all forms and does not recognize children born through it.

The drama began when the Indian government refused to give passports to the babies as they were not Indian nationals. As a result, the children began to be called 'stateless' and were in no-man's land, literally. Balaz had petitioned the Gujarat High Court (HC) to grant Indian citizenship to the babies so that they could travel out of the country to Germany. In its ruling, the HC had granted Indian citizenship to the twins in November 2009 on the basis of the 'natural' mother being an Indian The natural mother here was the Indian gestational surrogate, Martha Christy, who carried the babies. The HC took the definition of mother as being 'one who gives birth', thereby making the surrogate the legal mother of the children and thus the children Indians.

Dubbed as a 'landmark judgment' in the national press, the HC gave quasi legitimacy to the emotional tie that the gestational surrogate shared with the foetus during her pregnancy, and to the anonymous egg donor for her contribution to the conception and birth of the child. As per the Indian Constitution, citizenship is by birth, but through the Citizenship (Amendment) Act, 1986, an additional requirement was made which made it mandatory for one of the parents to hold an Indian passport/citizenship as well, over and above the clause of citizenship by birth. However, and this is interesting, the twins were also half Indian through their ties to the anonymous Indian woman who had donated her eggs to the arrangement. Despite this, the court recognized the act of gestation as qualifying motherhood, more than the tie through the genetic links of the egg or oocyte.

The Union of India, however, was unwilling to accept the idea of the mother as the 'one who gives birth', which is exactly what most surrogates were doing for foreign couples. This led to a situation wherein the government was unwilling to hand out passports and citizenship to non-Indian nationals, especially those whose parents were from countries where surrogacy is illegal. *It was only through extended inter-country negotiations between the Indian and German governments that led to a solution in this case in favour of the Balaz Twins being given temporary travel documents from the Indian government to go to Germany and pursue the citizenship case there.*

Stateless Commodities

In the Balaz Twins and Baby Manji cases, international negotiations oscillated between rescuing innocent stateless children and giving recognition to a practice that creates commodities of children. The Indian Supreme Court in its hearing of the Balaz case expressed concern by asking if 'an Indian baby is a commodity?' The court was concerned about the implied status of the children born from surrogacy as 'commodities', to be exchanged as part of a contractual agreement. The debate on statelessness seemed to blend in with the ethical question of 'creating' children through the exchange of money.

However, through the entire debate there never was any question raised in relation to the medical technology that made the entire arrangement possible in the first place. The focus was on the surrogate who was 'paid to relinquish' her rights over the child, and the differential notion of surrogacy in different countries and cultural contexts.

This was seen in the legal back and forth over the definition of 'mother'. After all, citizenship could be granted on the basis of one of the parents being an Indian by birth—; the Indian 'parent' in the TCGSA was usually the surrogate and in some cases the egg donor as well.

The cause for concern for the Indian state was two-fold: a population of unclaimed children in a country that already had a very bad track record in children's rights and the status of their Indian citizenship. The recurring fear of their becoming like 'discarded' beings for no fault of their own could only be changed with the granting of Indian citizenship which, however, meant that the Indian state compromised on its status as a sovereign.

This reluctance was part of the squeamishness associated with the monetary transaction which included child and technology. Accusations of illegal trafficking of children or 'baby selling' were made against the clinic and the IVF specialist who had helped Balaz have the twins. (That this clinic also ran a 'hostel' where pregnant surrogates were 'housed' away from their families for the period of nine months did not get as much attention in the legal proceedings.) Such accusations added to the discomfort that Indian courts felt on being faced with a situation where poor Indian women were renting their organs for money, verging on organ trafficking. The market rhetoric and the illegality attached to the underground marketplace of transnational surrogacy, which has as yet occupied a legally grey area, means that the entire arrangement, and the child born of it, is 'tainted'.

In many ways the Balaz and Manji cases came to map the ways in which states themselves operate in spheres that do not strictly adhere to boundaries and territories. Transnational adoption is the other relevant example as is immigration—both legal and illegal. The in-between spaces of ambiguity and 'fluid' laws often negotiate with the more formal processes of identity-giving and identity-making.

★★★

Transnational surrogacy occupies an ambiguous space legally and ethically. Despite varied legal debates, the intimate nature of the arrangement has led to questions regarding the moral valuations involved in giving legitimacy to the arrangement. Legally, the rights of the surrogate and the future child become the most important nodes of engagement.

Since 2018 the central government ministries have started provided maternity support to its female employees who commission a surrogacy arrangement. Thus, an employee who is 'pregnant' through a surrogate gets up to 180 days of paid maternity leave. This rule came about after a Delhi High Court order in 2015 asked all branches and departments of the government to extend maternity leave to an employee who has a child through surrogacy. Such an order brings in additional elements of institutional support and care in relation to surrogacy, which cannot be subsumed within debates of a ban. The legal issues of surrogacy with respect to its actual practice is complicated and requires active consideration of all participants involved.

This chapter brought some of the 'sticky' issues regarding the surrogate and the child to the fore. The importance of engaging with existing legislation to pave the way for more equitable rights makes it imperative, ethically and morally, that future legislation for surrogacy in India focuses on the regulation of the surrogacy arrangement.

6

Conclusion

As we come to the end of this short introduction to surrogacy in India, some of the major ideas within the study of commercial surrogacy resonate with our chapter focus areas—transnationalism, altruism, and labour. In the previous chapters, commercial surrogacy has been the focus in its transnational avatar and as an exclusively gestational arrangement. Of importance is the notion of 'altruism' that is an important element of contemporary surrogacy arrangement and how it has come to influence the idea of surrogacy in India and internationally. Similarly, the surrogate has remained an important element in the conversation on reproductive rights and ethics.

A book on transnational commercial surrogacy that has looked at its contemporary avatar cannot ignore its past trajectory and future imaginings. Thus, in the conclusion, I bring the focus back to how surrogacy as a practice has come to mark feminist conversations about the body and reproduction. Ending this book with a brief, albeit necessary, look at feminist conversation means that the woman at the centre of the arrangement—the surrogate—remains key to our understanding of how the surrogacy arrangement is ultimately understood.

Reproductive Politics

Exercising control over reproduction was part of the Cold War agenda that included citizens, nation states, and feminists. Spurring the production, control, and distribution of technologies that began with preventing conception were both feminist organizations and international NGOs, who brought them to the developing world of South Asia through the support of global and local governments. The ways in which reproductive technologies came to mark feminist engagements can be seen in their changing positions vis-à-vis the ideological support or criticism extended to NRTs/ARTs. Mapped into two primary phases, 1984–91 and 1999–2000, the feminist 'text' on NRTs has been constantly evolving (Thompson 2008).

During the first phase, responses oscillated between the radical and liberal feminist stances on the technologies and their impact on women's bodies and identities. This

118

is particularly marked in the position taken by Shulamith Firestone, who saw reproductive technologies as liberatory. Her point of view was completely opposite to the position articulated by Maria Mies, whose critique of reproductive technologies places them within eugenic politics that aim to exploit and usurp women's reproductive potential for the production of suitable, gendered, and racial bodies (discussed in detail later). Liberal feminism sees surrogacy in itself as the true form of exercising the right to choice. To be able to decide to be pregnant for someone else is a truly liberating step forward. However, the exercising of reproductive choice is not a privilege that many poor, disadvantaged women can make. The liberal feminist arguments in favour of surrogacy have been critiqued by noting that the right to choice does not exist when the woman does not have the luxury to exercise it. Interestingly, this framework is invoked in the case of commercial surrogacy with some feminist scholars going as far as to say that surrogacy should be restricted to its altruistic form.

The second phase of feminist studies of reproductive technologies also began to engage with non-Western experiences of women, and men, to understand their voices and agency within an otherwise monolithic representation of technologies as 'male' and invasive. The globalization of reproductive technologies and services has to some extent brought back the criticisms and representations that formed the core of the feminist text in the 'first' phase. This is largely due to the increasing commercialization and commodification of the woman's body—now 'disassembled' and marketed into so many parts that its essence seems to be lost. Creating an empty space out of women's reproductive bodies is a characteristic of ARTs—that disassemble a single body into many parts—each one exchangeable in a global reproductive market

The debate on reproductive choice and justice has gained from the multiple narratives of women exercising different reproductive choices. Cross-cultural differences that inform feminist dialogues and methodologies are also indicative of differences within cultures. Feminists from the developing world have found this to be the most telling—so much so that the 'poverty of choice' has also often been framed within a perspective that is in turn focused on the women of developing or poor countries of Asia and Africa. Ethnographic explorations in the area of reproductive choices or the lack of it have time and again reiterated this and led to the formulation of the idea of 'stratified reproduction'. This involves the exploitation of women by women in contexts of geographical and economic power differences. Thus, women from the Third World/developing world/Global South are constantly asked to provide reproductive services in the form of nannies or surrogates to women in the developed world or Global North.

Both liberal and fundamentalist feminist views regarding ARTs are part of a rhetoric that does not look at the experiences of the women undergoing procedures that emerge from these technologies. However, to a large extent this 'rhetoric' helped social theory re-engage with gender and women's issues—bringing reproduction to the 'centre of social theory'.

The Marxist–Feminist critique of reproductive technologies places them within a 'mode of procreation' that are dependent upon complicating ideas linked to reproductive labour by mixing them with those of eulogized motherhood. In that sense, for Marxist-Feminism the surrogate's labour has to be recognized as such, rather than hiding it within the complicated rhetoric of sacrifice and altruism.

In the end the commoditization of reproductive bodies and selves is a taken-for-granted process of increasing industrialization and lower equity. Transnational commercial surrogacy represents this change in very stark terms. However, the dynamism and the varied levels of engagement within the surrogacy arrangement continue to provoke discussions and debates for future research.

References

Berend, Zsuzsa. 2010. 'Surrogate Losses: Understanding of Pregnancy Loss and Assisted Reproduction Among Surrogate Mothers'. *Medical Anthropology Quarterly* 24 (2), 240–62.

Bharadwaj, Aditya. 2000. 'How Some Indian Baby Makers Are Made: Media Narratives and Assisted Conception in India'. *Anthropology and Medicine* 7 (1), 63–78.

———. 2002. 'Conception Politics: Medical Egos, Media Spotlights, and the Context over Test-Tube Firsts in India'. In *Infertility Around the Globe: New Thinking on Childlessness, Gender, Reproductive Technologies*, edited by Marcia C. Inhorn and Frank Van Balen, pp. 315–33. Berkeley: University of California Press.

———. 2003. 'Why Adoption Is Not an Option in India: The Visibility of Infertility, the Secrecy of Donor Insemination, and Other Cultural Complexities'. *Social Science and Medicine* 56 (9), 1867–80.

———. 2016. *Conceptions: Infertility and Procreative Technologies in India*, vol. 34. New York: Berghahn Books.

Bharadwaj, Aditya, and Peter Glasner. 2009. *Local Cells, Global Science: The Rise of Embryonic Stem Cell Research in India*. New Delhi: Routledge.

Butler, Judith. 2002. 'Is Kinship Always Already Heterosexual?'. *Differences: A Journal of Feminist Cultural Studies* 13 (1), 14–44.

Chatterjee, Ayesha, and Sally Wheelan. 2017. 'Frequently Unasked Questions: Understanding and Responding to Gaps in Public Knowledge of International Surrogacy Practices Worldwide'. In *Babies for Sale: Transnational Surrogacy, Human Rights and the Politics of Reproduction*, edited by Miranda Davies, pp. 221–44. London: Zed Books.

CII (Confederation of Indian Industries)–McKinsey. 2002. *Healthcare in India: The Road Ahead*. Report by CII and McKinsey & Co.

Deepa, V., Mohan Rao, Rama Baru, Ramila Bisht, N. Sarojini, and S.F. Murray. 2013. *Sourcing Surrogates: Actors, Agencies and Networks*. New Delhi: Zubaan Publishing Services.

Deomampo, Daisy. 2016. *Transnational Reproduction: Race, Kinship and Commercial Surrogacy in India*. New York: NYU Press.

Gimenez, Martha E. 1991. 'The Mode of Reproduction in Transition: A Marxist-Feminist Analysis of the Effects of Reproductive Technologies'. *Gender and Society* 5 (3), 334–50.

Hochschild, Arlie. 2011. 'Emotional Life on the Market Frontier'. *Annual Review of Sociology* 37, 21–33.

Indian Council of Medical Research (ICMR). 2010. *The Assisted Reproductive Technologies (Regulation) Bill*. New Delhi: Ministry of Health and Family Welfare, Government of India.

Inhorn, Marcia. 2015. *Cosmopolitan Conceptions: IVF Sojourns in Global Dubai*. Durham, NC: Duke University Press.

Inhorn, Marcia, and Daphne Birenbaum-Carmeli. 2008. 'Assisted Reproductive Technologies and Cultural Change'. *Annual Review of Anthropology* 37, 177–96.

Krolokke, Charlotte, and S. Pant. 2012. '"I Only Need Her Uterus": Neo-Liberal Discourses on Transnational Surrogacy'. *NORA: Nordic Journal of Feminist and Gender Research* 20 (4), 233–48.

Law Commission of India. 2009. *Report No. 228: Need for Legislation to Regulate Assisted Reproductive Technology Clinics as well as Rights and Obligations of Parties to a Surrogacy*. New Delhi: Government of India.

Levine, Hal B. 2003. 'Gestational Surrogacy: Nature and Culture in Kinship'. *Ethnology* 42 (3), 173–85.

Majumdar, Anindita. 2017. *Transnational Commercial Surrogacy and the (Un)Making of Kin in India*. New Delhi: Oxford University Press.

———. 2018. Conceptualizing Surrogacy as Work-Labour: Domestic Labour in Commercial Gestational Surrogacy in India. *Journal of South Asian Development* 13 (2), 210–27.

Markens, Susan. 2007. *Surrogate Motherhood and the Politics of Reproduction*. Berkeley: University of California Press.

Menon, Nivedita. 2012. *Seeing Like a Feminist*. New Delhi: Penguin.

Mody, Pervez. 2008. The Intimate State: Love, Marriage and Law in India. London: Routledge.

Nadimpally, Sarojini, and Anindita Majumdar (2017). 'Recruiting to Give Birth: Agent-Facilitators and the Commercial Surrogacy Arrangement in India'. In *Babies for Sale: Transnational Surrogacy, Human Rights and the Politics of Reproduction*, edited by Miranda Davies, pp. 65–81. London: Zed Books.

Nandy, Amrita. 2017. *Motherhood and Choice: Uncommon Mothers, Childfree Women*. New Delhi: Zubaan and New Text.

Pande, Amrita. 2009. '"It May Be Her Eggs, But It's My Blood": Surrogates and Everyday Forms of Kinship in India'. *Qualitative Sociology* 32 (4), 379–97.

———. 2010. Commercial Surrogacy in India: Manufacturing a Perfect Mother-Worker. *Signs: Journal of Women in Culture and Society* 35 (4), 969–992.

———. 2011. 'Transnational Commercial Surrogacy in India: Gifts for Global Sisters?' *Reproductive BioMedicine Online* 23 (5), 618–25.

———. 2014. *Wombs in Labor: Transnational Commercial Surrogacy in India*. New York: Columbia University Press.

Parker, P.J. 1983. 'Motivation of Surrogate Mothers—Initial Findings'. *American Journal of Psychiatry*, 140 (1), 117–18.

Parliamentary Standing Committee (PSC). 2017. *102nd Report on The Surrogacy (Regulation) Bill, 2016*. New Delhi: Rajya Sabha Secretariat.

Ragone, Helena. 1994. *Surrogate Motherhood: Conception in the Heart*. Boulder, CO: Westview Press.

———. 1996. 'Chasing the Blood Tie: Surrogate Mothers, Adoptive Mothers and Fathers'. *American Ethnologist* 23 (2), 352–65.

Rao, Mohan. 2012. 'Why All Non-Altruistic Surrogacy Should be Banned'. *Economic and Political Weekly*, XLVII (15), 15–17.

Rapp, Rayna. 2011. 'Reproductive Entanglements: Body, State, and Culture in the Dys/Regulation of Childbearing'. *Social Research* 78 (3), 693–718.

Reddy, S., and Imrana Qadeer. 2010. 'Medical Tourism in India: Progress or Predicament?'. *Economic and Political Weekly* 45 (20), 69–75.

Riggs, Damien, and Clemence Due. 2017. 'Constructions of Gay Men's Reproductive Desires on Commercial Surrogacy Websites'. In *Babies for Sale: Transnational Commercial Surrogacy, Human Rights and the Politics of Reproduction*, edited by Miranda Davies, pp. 33–45. London: Zed Books.

Rudrappa, Sharmila. 2015. *Discounted Life: The Price of Global Surrogacy in India*. New York: NYU Press.

Sama. 2009. 'Assisted Reproductive Technologies: For Whose Benefit?'. *Economic and Political Weekly* 44 (18), 25–31.

———. 2010. 'Critique of the Draft Assisted Reproductive Technologies (Regulation) Bill & Rules–2008'. In *Making Babies: Birth Markets and Assisted Reproductive Technologies in India*, edited by Sandhya Srinivasan, pp. 126–38. New Delhi: Zubaan.

———. 2012. *Birthing a Market: A Study of Commercial Surrogacy in India*. New Delhi: Sama Resource Group for Women and Health.

Saravanan, Sheela. 2010. 'Transnational Surrogacy and the Objectification of Gestational Mothers'. *Economic and Political Weekly* XLV (16), 25–8.

Sarojini, N., Anindita Majumdar, Veena Johari, and Priya Ranjan. 2015. 'Branding Mother India'. *Kafila*, 24 May. Available at: https://kafila.online/tag/dentsu-mama-lab/, last accessed on 4 May 2018.

Speier, Amy. 2016. *Fertility Holidays: IVF Tourism and the Reproduction of Whiteness*. New York: NYU Press.

Thompson, Charis. 2005. *Making Parents: The Ontological Choreography of Reproductive Technologies*. Cambridge, Massachusetts: MIT Press.

———. 2008. 'Fertile Ground: Feminists Theorize Reproductive Technologies'. In *Technology Studies: Technology and Culture*, edited by Rayvon Fouche, vol. IV, pp. 260–80. London: Sage.

Vora, Kalindi. 2013. 'Potential, Risk and Return in Transnational Indian Gestational Surrogacy. *Current Anthropology* 54 (7), S97–S106.

Weston, Kath. 1991. *Families We Choose: Lesbians, Gays, Kinship*. New York: Columbia University Press.

Further Readings

To understand the myth of Krishna's birth from the perspective of assisted conception, Andre Couture (2009) is a helpful entry point. (Couture, Andre. 2009. 'The Story of Samkarsana's and Krsna's Births: A Drama Involving Embryos'. In *Imagining the Fetus: The Unborn in Myth, Religion and Culture*, edited by Vanessa R. Sasson and Jane Marie Law, pp. 11–31. New York: Oxford University Press.)

Miranda Davies' (2017) book is also a ready reference for contemporary problems related to commercial surrogacy. (Davies, Miranda, ed. 2017. *Babies for Sale: Transnational Surrogacy, Human Rights and the Politics of Reproduction*. London: Zed Books.)

For the discussion on reproductive politics, Robyn Rowland's (1992) work on IVF and its impact on women's bodies is an excellent starting point. (Rowland, Robyn. 1992. *Living Laboratories: Women and Reproductive Technologies*. Sydney: Pan Macmillan.)

Some other works to refer are:

Carney, Scott. 2010. 'Cash on Delivery'. *The Caravan*, September, 62–8.

Oza, N. 2010. 'Cash on Delivery'. *The Week*, June 13, 20–3.

Teman, Elly. 2008. 'The Social Construction of Surrogacy Research: An Anthropological Critique of the Psychosocial Scholarship on Surrogate Motherhood'. *Social Science and Medicine* 67 (7), 1104–12.

Index

About the Author

Anindita Majumdar is assistant professor, Department of Liberal Arts, Indian Institute of Technology, Hyderabad, India. She has recently published *Transnational Commercial Surrogacy and the (Un)Making of Kin in India*, based on her research on commercial surrogacy in India. Currently, Anindita is researching ageing and its linkages with assisted reproduction. She has published in journals such as *Contemporary South Asia*, *Indian Journal of Gender Studies*, *Gender, Technology and Development*, *Journal of South Asian Development,* and others. Anindita has previously taught at University of Delhi, Manipal University, Karnataka, and Indian Institute of Technology Delhi.